SHEFFIELD'S SHOCKING PAST

Published by ACM Retro Ltd,
The Grange,
Church Street,
Dronfield,
Sheffield S18 1QB.

Visit ACM Retro at:
www.acmretro.com

A catalogue record for this book is available from the British Library.

SHEFFIELD'S SHOCKING PAST

Forgotten Tales of Murder, Mishap and Gruesome Misdemeanour

Part 1 – The Victorian City

By Chris Hobbs and Matthew Bell

TERRIBLE ACCIDENT. SHEFFIELD—CHILDREN TRAMPLED TO DEATH.

MURDER OF A WIFE AND FOUR CHILDREN AT SHEFFIELD.

CONTENTS

INTRODUCTION

Anybody who has ever undertaken an internet search of any of the following terms:

Murders in Sheffield; Victorian Sheffield; Sheffield workhouse; Accidents in Sheffield; Sheffield executions

and other similar subjects will have seen listed high up in the results the website *www.chrishobbs.com*, which is a goldmine of information relating to innumerable aspects of the history of Sheffield. This book is based on the extensive research undertaken by Chris Hobbs – a life-long resident of Sheffield – for his website, and is intended to provide a window, albeit a very small one, on to a few of the more gruesome and grizzly episodes in the annals of the city.

What this is not intended to be is a comprehensive study of the whole catalogue of murders, fatal accidents and other such tragic incidents that have ever occurred in Sheffield, but it gives an insight into some of the unusual, little known and downright bizarre events that happened during the Victorian period. It somehow seems appropriate that the first judicial execution to take place in Victoria's long reign was that of a Sheffield man who murdered another Sheffield man. At the other end of the scale, both in terms of years and outcome, one of the last murders to be committed in Sheffield during the Victorian era remained unsolved; the man charged with the crime was acquitted at trial and the perpetrator of the offence was never found. In addition to the various murderous crimes of rage, jealousy and greed described in the following chapters, there are quirky stories, tear-jerking stories, incredible stories and stories that would be hilarious if they weren't so sad.

It is surprising – though on second thoughts perhaps it isn't – that many of the events described here revolve around the public house and the consumption of alcohol, often in prodigious quantities, by both men and women, at all hours of the day and night. In much of nineteenth century Sheffield, the quality of the beer was more reliable than the quality of the drinking water. It was cheap too, affordable to even the poorest classes, but frequently purchased to excess and at the expense of the basic necessities of life, such as food and fuel. Some of the pub names you will recognise, but many of them are long gone. There is much discussion in modern Britain about binge drinking and the abuse of alcohol, but after you have read what follows you will probably come to the conclusion that it is nothing new.

Something else you may recognise are the names of streets. The street names, and their locations, have rarely changed in the past two hundred years, but the environment around them certainly has. The central districts of Victorian Sheffield – and well into the twentieth century for that matter – were the home of grime, pollution, poverty, densely packed slum housing and 'little mesters' workshops. Many of the tales you will read here are centred on that grim area where the only refuge its inhabitants had from drab employment – if they were lucky – and the constant battle to scrape together enough money to eat and keep warm was to be found in drink. When the mind and body were numb, nothing else mattered, for a short time anyway. However, bad things were not confined simply to the poor, working-class areas of the city. There are enough instances of tragedy in better-off suburbs of the city to realise that life could be fragile in these areas too.

Another aspect of Sheffield life that is a permanent fixture throughout these tales is the type of employment held down by the city's poorer inhabitants. Sheffield was a major centre of cutlery and light tool manufacture, and the jobs that keep cropping up in the reports show that the number of men employed in these trades was enormous. Read on and you might believe that every male in Sheffield was a table blade grinder, a table knife hafter, a knife handle presser, a hammer grinder or an edge tool grinder. Sheffield's status as a world leader in table-wear and hand-tool production was indeed not a myth. This was a time of hopelessness for many, as work may only be held sporadically, if any work was available at all. A home may consist of only two rooms (some only one), in which a family of seven or eight would cook (if they had anything to cook, and some fuel to make a fire), eat, wash (if they had water) and sleep, often on filthy and damp straw mattresses and in the same ragged clothes they wore during the day. If they were lucky they might have had a couple of beds, and it was a time when two men would sleep together without any sexual connotations. That is what was done; it was normal.

As well as recognising the names of streets and public houses, you may also recognise the names of people and, indeed, particular addresses. You may have undertaken some genealogy work and now find a name you know from your research. You may see an address and think, 'I know someone who used to live there,' or even, 'I live there!' It is not beyond the realms of possibility that you are related to a murder victim, or a murderer, or that you sleep every night in a house in which someone met their untimely end. Hopefully that will not force you into moving house, but instead cause you to embrace the historical significance of your humble abode. Even if you do not live close to where something terrible once happened, take a walk to one of the locations and let yourself go. Walk to the top of White Croft, or Smithfield, or Boden Lane, or Silver Street, which all lie in a small area a short distance from the city centre, close your eyes and imagine what each place would have been like over a hundred years ago. It is only in your head, but it is an evocative picture.

It is noticeable how much the writing style in newspaper reports has altered over the years, and, indeed, how the meaning of certain words has changed; such as the legal terms 'to prosecute' and 'to execute'. Today, a person is said to be prosecuted for an alleged criminal offence. In fact, it is not the person that is prosecuted, but the case against him. Today, the legal killing of a person (in countries that still employ capital punishment) is called an execution. This too is incorrect. It is not the person that is executed, but in the first place the law, then the sentence; in other words, it means 'to carry out'. If a judge passes a death sentence, he is therefore executing the law to its fullest extent. Consequently, the hangman does not carry out an execution, he carries out (i.e. he executes) the death sentence. Another one is the 'post mortem'. In modern times these words define the examination of a dead body. In fact, the term should not be used as a noun, but an adjective: 'post-mortem examination', i.e. an examination made 'post mortem', or 'after death'. Victorian newspapers used these two words in their correct manner.

On a more prosaic level, if today you are said to be 'excited', you are either really looking forward to something or have experienced something that gave you a great thrill. However, in the nineteenth century the word meant simply 'agitated' – a crowd of onlookers at or participants in a particular event became 'excited' not because they enjoyed what they were witnessing or taking part in, but because they were overtaken by the emotion of the scene or by their convictions that what they were doing was right. Another is the phrase 'more or less'. Today it means 'about' or 'approximately', but a hundred years ago, if a number of people were 'more or less seriously injured', it meant simply that some were more seriously injured than others, some were less seriously injured than others. There are also words that have 'more or less' fallen out of use, such as 'whither' and 'thither', whilst people were 'removed' to the mortuary or hospital, not 'taken'. A child was usually termed 'it' rather than 'he' or 'she', a usage that might not be deemed acceptable today. It was mentioned earlier that street names have not changed. Well, that is only partially correct, in that they haven't, but they have. Newspaper reports would not state 'West Street' but 'West-street', and not 'Glossop Road' but 'the Glossop road'. 'Today' and 'tomorrow' were 'to-day' and 'to-morrow'. When the modern descriptions came into being is unknown, but it was probably surprisingly recent. In this book the modern usage has been employed throughout.

One other surprising aspect of newspaper reports of crimes was the presumption of guilt; the word 'alleged' was hardly used. A man accused of killing somebody was rarely described as 'the alleged murderer', but merely as 'the murderer'. In fact he wasn't even 'the accused', he was 'the prisoner', which implied guilt. The facts of the case were exactly that – the facts of the case, whether or not they had been proven in court. If they were in the newspaper report, they were fact. Presumably the prospect of a newspaper being the subject of legal action, or that its reports might lead to an unfair trial, did not enter the editor's head. Such occurrences were a thing of the future. Reports often claimed to know the exact goings on in a house or a street in the moments before a tragic event took place; for example how the victim or 'prisoner' felt and the precise movements he made in the build-up to a crime, despite never having talked to him. Did they make it up, elaborating, embellishing and extrapolating as if they were writing a novel in order to 'liven up' the story? It certainly appears so sometimes, even though the events that were known to be true were frequently incredible enough in themselves. It also appears that, on occasion, reporters were allowed full access to both the scene of a crime and to official reports of injuries, so detailed are the descriptions.

What also has to be remembered is that cases were almost exclusively decided on witness statements or confessions. Forensic science was in its infancy; there were no fingerprints, no DNA, not even blood matching. If there was blood on a knife or a hammer, it was presumed to be the blood of the victim, and therefore it was the murder weapon. The science involved extended to the opinion and constrained findings of 'medical men', especially at inquests. If a

8

medical man stated in court that something in particular had occurred, he was believed without question.

However, despite the often 'primitive' nature of criminal investigations, the order and method of the subsequent judicial proceedings may surprise, albeit that inquests were often held in pubs and the bodies of murder victims were put on public display! This was a period of poor literacy and sparse education so news was passed by word of mouth and things had to be seen to be believed – literally. The public's interest in morbid events was such that any newsworthy story spread rapidly, grabbing the public attention so readily that those who could read pored over lengthy newspaper reports and funerals of murder or accident victims often attracted hundreds or even thousands of fascinated spectators.

At the same time, however, inquests and trials were strictly regimented and meticulously recorded, and were indistinguishable from what goes on today. In this regard, the more things change, the more they stay the same.

CHAPTER 1

THE HANGING OF THOMAS WILLIAMS, 1837

'Let me warn you all of the demon drink!'

From 1837 to 1901 Queen Victoria reigned over the world's biggest empire, and during her 64-year reign approximately 1,100 judicial hangings were carried out in Great Britain and Ireland. The *Preston Chronicle* of August 5, 1837 reported on the first to be held in England during Victoria's time on the throne. It was another first for Sheffield!

WILLIAMS THE MURDERER
Mr Justice Coltman departed from York on Friday afternoon, for Durham: his Lordship left Thomas Williams convicted of murder in Sheffield, for execution. The unfortunate man will suffer the extreme penalty of the law on Saturday the 5th of August.

A fuller report appeared in the Sheffield press:

MURDER AT SHEFFIELD.—Yesterday week an in-
quest was held at Sheffield, on the body of — Froggatt, basket-maker who had been murdered by Thomas Williams

William Biggins, examined: 'On Friday, the 17th of March last, the prisoner invited me to a public house, and whilst we were drinking together he said, "I have a point in view, and if I can accomplish it, I will make you a present of my shears, as I shall never use them any more. I intend to smash Froggatt's brains out this night." It was concerning work that he would do. Between 4 and 5 o'clock the prisoner left the house for a few minutes, and on his return said, "I have done it, I have killed old Frog." He had had liquor, but was not drunk; he appeared to know what he was doing and saying.'

Froggatt lingered until the 6th of April. John Waterfall, jun., constable, deposed to the following conversation on the prisoner's apprehension: 'I told him that I was a constable, and that it was my duty to take him into custody. He said, "Very well, I will go with you. If he dies, I shall be satisfied; but if not, I shall be sorry." I said, "You had better not say anything about it," but as we walked along he said, "B—t him! If he dies it will be a good thing for trade. He was a damned rascal, and he wanted to take the bread off my trencher. If I have not killed him, it is a pity. B—t him! If I have but killed him, the trade will have the benefit of it. I care nothing about myself; if I have not killed him, and am to be punished for that, I shall be grieved."'

The jury unhesitatingly returned a verdict of 'Wilful Murder', and the prisoner was committed to York Castle.

A later report gave details of the trial:

MURDER AT SHEFFIELD
Thomas Williams (29), was charged with the wilful murder of Thomas Froggatt, of Sheffield, on the 29th of March last. The prisoner refused to plead, and the Judge directed a plea of 'Not Guilty' to be recorded. Counsel for the prosecution, Mr D. Dundas and Mr Wortley; for the prisoner, Mr Bliss. Mr Dundas stated the case to the jury, which will be found detailed by the following witnesses.

William Jeffreys deposed that he was a basket-maker, and was in the service of Mr Moore, of Sheffield. The deceased was in his service also, and had been so for a fortnight before this affair happened. The prisoner was also in the service of Mr Moore, and had been so about three months before the murder was committed. On the Wednesday before this took place, witness was with the prisoner at Lindley's public house, and had some conversation with him. The prisoner said he thought that Froggatt had been asking for his work, and that in consequence he should leave. He went off drinking on Tuesday, the day before this conversation took place, and did not return to work after. On Friday, the 7th of March, witness was at work in the shop, as was also the deceased. There was no person in the shop except himself and Froggatt. Prisoner came in about half drunk, and asked for his shears, but not finding them went out, and after an absence of about half an hour he came back. The deceased still continued working. Prisoner again inquired for his shears, sought for them, but could not find them. He was then on the right-hand side of Froggatt, whom he immediately struck over the right side of the head with a hedging bill. The prisoner said, 'Damn him, I'll finish him,' and saying this, he struck him again with the same weapon. Witness ran out to Mr Moore's house. Prisoner came out of the shop about half a minute after. Prisoner then went to Lindley's public house. Witness and a person by the name of William Biggins, then went into the shop to assist Froggatt.

William Biggins deposed that he was a basket-maker at Sheffield, and knew the prisoner. On the 17th of March last he came to witness's lodgings, and asked him if he would go and take a glass of ale at the Black Swan, adding that he had been there since nine o'clock in the morning. They went to the Black Swan, and sat drinking there for two hours, when they entered into conversation respecting some shears. The prisoner repeated he had a point in view several times, and witness repeatedly asked him what it was, when he answered that he intended to mash Frogatt's brains out that night. Witness said, 'I cannot think of such a thing, Tom,' to which he replied, 'I can.' Witness asked him what he was going to do it for, to which he replied, that it was about work. No further conversation took place there after that. Prisoner then asked witness if he could take a walk, and he would fetch him the shears. They immediately went to Thomas Lindley's public house, which is very near the workshops, and had some ale to drink. The prisoner went out twice into the yard which leads to the workshops, saying he would go and look for the shears. He was not away above five or six minutes, when he came back and said, 'I have done it.' Witness asked him what he had done. To which he replied, 'I have killed old Froggatt.' There were three or four persons in the kitchen when he said this. After the prisoner said he had killed Froggatt, Jeffreys came in by the yard door, went towards the prisoner, and looking at witness said, 'He has killed old Froggatt.' He and Jeffreys left the prisoner in the house, and went into the workshop, where the deceased was laid, his head covered with blood, but he was alive: witness saw the hedging-bill, which was bloody. He then went back to Lindley's public house, and said to prisoner, 'Tom, he is alive – you have not killed him.' He said, 'If I thought I had not, I would go back and give him another chop.' Witness said, 'Tom, they will hang you as sure as you are born.' He replied, 'I don't care a damn, they may hang me, and now, if Froggatt is dead.' He also added, 'It would be a benefit to trade if he was dead.' The prisoner was neither drunk nor sober.

George Moore, jun., deposed that he is the son of Mr Moore, basket-maker, Sheffield. The prisoner came to his father's house on Friday afternoon and asked witness if he had seen anything of his shears. Witness said he had not, when the prisoner told him his father had fetched them out of the shop. Prisoner then said, 'George, I have something on my mind that hurts me much,' and added that his father must take care of himself that night or he (prisoner) should play him a trick. Witness asked him what trick it was, but prisoner would not tell him, saying he should keep that to himself. Witness's father then came in, and denied having seen anything of the prisoner's shears.

George Moore, sen., basket-maker, Sheffield, in whose employ the prisoner had been for nine or ten weeks, deposed that he had not been at work for three or four days before the murder was committed. The deceased had also been in his employ a few weeks, but when he gave him work, he did not know of any quarrel between him and the prisoner. Witness was in Lindley's public house when the prisoner came in, and upon seeing witness he said, 'I have finished him: if I had not finished him, I should go back and finish him.' Witness told him he was a villain if he had done so, when he replied, 'If you are not off I will finish you also.' Witness asked him what for, to which he replied, 'For setting another man to do my work.' Witness told him he had not done that, there was plenty of work for him if he would attend to it.

Mr Chesman deposed that he was a surgeon at Sheffield. He went to the shop of Mr Moore to see the deceased. He found him lying on the floor, exceedingly faint, and bleeding very much from the head. He restrained the haemorrhage, applied bandages, rolled his head carefully up, and directed him to be taken to the Infirmary. There was a large wound extending from the right side of the crown of the head to the middle of the temple, and when witness had wiped away the blood, he could see the wound was very open, and that the brain was out. There were two slight wounds on the left side of the head. Witness was present after his death to examine the head, and Mr Jackson, who had attended to him at the Infirmary, was with witness. They examined the skull, and found it had penetrated through about four inches; the brain had also been penetrated. In his opinion the wound was the cause of death.

Mr Bliss made a very ingenious speech for the prisoner, during which he endeavoured to show the jury that the conduct of the prisoner evinced insanity, and that the insanity was irritated by the quantity of liquor which he had taken. The Learned Judge in the most careful manner went through the evidence, and remarked to the jury the total absence of any proof of insanity of the prisoner. The jury retired for a few minutes and returned into court with a verdict of 'Guilty'. His Lordship then proceeded in a very affecting manner, to pass sentence of death on the prisoner, exhorting him to employ the short period he should live in this world in humble supplication to the throne of grace for mercy. The prisoner stood quite firm; when his Lordship repeated the prayer 'May the Lord God Almighty have mercy upon your soul', the prisoner closed his eyes and very fervently uttered 'Amen'.

Froggatt had taken three weeks to die from his head wounds. A report of Williams's execution, which took place on August 12, 1837 (for some reason a week later than scheduled), stated:

'Let me warn you all of the demon drink!' proclaimed Thomas Williams, 29, as he stood on the scaffold outside York Prison on Saturday, August 12th, 1837. The crowd, said to be 'disappointingly small', who had come to watch him hang, made no discernible response. Williams killed a workmate, Thomas Froggatt, in a ferocious attack at the little factory in Silver Street, Sheffield, where they were both employed as basket makers. Williams, who certainly had a drink problem, had been hired by the factory-owner, and believed Froggatt was after his work. He stabbed Froggatt with a sharpened billhook used to cut willows, then embedded it in his skull. While another work colleague ran screaming into the street, Williams calmly walked off to the Windsor Castle pub, had a drink, and waited for the police.

This report clears up where exactly the murderous assault took place. The Black Swan pub is the one that still stands on Snig Hill (opened in 1774 and more recently known as the Boardwalk music venue), and Thomas Lindley's pub is given its proper name of the Windsor Castle, which Douglas Lamb's book *A Pub On Every Corner* states stood at No.21 Silver Street (opened 1833, closed 1896). The men must have walked along Bank Street and Queen Street. There are no old buildings remaining on Silver Street so it is impossible to be certain where No.21 was situated.

It's not the same building, but a Black Swan pub has stood here for more than 175 years (photograph 2011)

Another report, this time from the *York Herald*, added further detail:

On Saturday, the 12th instant, at noon, the last sentence of the law was executed on Thomas Williams, convicted at the Yorkshire Assizes of the wilful murder of Thomas Froggatt, of Sheffield. The testimony of guilt was clear and convincing, the unhappy culprit having been brought to an ignominious and untimely end from a malicious principle of revenge which he had harboured in his breast. He had a wife and five children, but we have not heard that they visited him since his trial. At an early hour in the morning he was removed from the condemned cell to the press room, where he engaged in prayer with the ordinary. He appeared fully impressed with the conviction that he was about to enter the presence of his eternal Judge; and said his deepest grief was that his wife, who was innocent, would be the greatest sufferer. When he had again fervently engaged in prayer, he turned his face to the crowd, and in a distinct voice, and with a collected manner, said: 'Fellow-men, you are come to witness a spectacle of intemperance – an awful scene. I hope this will make a lasting impression upon every soul before me. A man in the prime of life, 30 years of age, cut off through this diabolical crime of intemperance. Is there a drunkard before me? Yes, I see many. Let him go home, and be so no more. Is there a liar? Let him speak truth for the future, and turn to God with full purpose of heart. I have to inform you that I am leaving a grateful partner behind me; one that is walking in the commandments of the Lord, and one that delights in her God.'

The fatal bolt was drawn. He struggled very little, and after hanging the usual time, his body was buried within the precincts of the prison.

Silver Street in 2011

CHAPTER 2

ALFRED PRIMROSE AND ELIZABETH THORNHILL, CROOKESMOOR, 1838

'He laughed at her, and used some very unkind and undeserving expressions towards her'

On March 1, 1818, Alfred Primrose, the son of Daniel and Martha Primrose, was christened in what is now Sheffield Cathedral. Just over seven months later on September 26, 1818, Elizabeth Thornhill, the daughter of George and Ann Thornhill, was christened in the same church.

Twenty years later, the following report appeared in *The Times* on January 5, 1838, describing an inquest that took place at the Crookesmoor Workhouse the previous Tuesday. Crookesmoor Workhouse no longer exists but an old map shows its position to be adjacent to Crookesmoor Road and not far from Crookesmoor Dam. The inquest was inquiring into the sudden death of nineteen-year-old Elizabeth Thornhill.

On Tuesday afternoon last an inquest was held by Mr. Badger, Coroner, and a respectable jury, at the Crookes Moor workhouse, on view of the body of a fine young woman, 19 years of age, called Elizabeth Thornhill, a straw bonnet maker, residing in Rockingham-lane, Sheffield, and the eldest of 12 children.

It appeared from the evidence that the deceased had kept company for nearly three years with a young man named Alfred Primrose, an ivory cutter by trade, by whom she was pregnant; that he had treated her harshly, and about 1 o'clock on Friday last had met her in the High Street, laughed at her, and used some very unkind and undeserving expressions towards her. This conduct seemed to press heavily on her mind, and she went home in the greatest distress, cut off part of her hair, which she enclosed in a tortoiseshell box, with a locket, watch-guard, comb, some letters, and other articles, and gave them to her sister, telling her, if Primrose did not call for the articles, she was to take them to him at 6 o'clock that night; and that he would have to rue for what he had done to her, if he ever rued in his life. From that time the deceased was not seen again until her lifeless body was found in the dam. Evidence was adduced showing that the deceased had for more than three months not been so lively as usual, but much depressed in her spirits, and the jury, under all the circumstances, and after strongly reprimanding Primrose for his unkind and unfeeling conduct towards the deceased, returned a verdict of 'Found drowned, having, while in a state of temporary derangement, thrown herself into Crookes Moor Dam.'

The *Sheffield and Rotherham Independent* also covered the inquest, which heard from a witness, Lydia Maude. The witness explained that she was returning from Sheffield, down the Tobacco Walk, the previous Friday about five o'clock when she heard screams. As she had frequently heard similar screams at night she did not take any notice, but mentioned what she had heard when she arrived at Mr Oddy's public house. Another witness, George Hall, stated that as he was walking with his dog in a field adjoining the dam he saw something like a bonnet or a cloak in the water. He sent his dog into the dam to retrieve it, and when it did so Hall saw the hand of a woman appear above the water. He immediately shouted an alarm and, assisted by another man, the body was pulled from the dam and taken to the workhouse.

So this 'fine young woman' died what only can be termed a tragic death. But what was interesting was the strong reprimand that was issued by the jury to Alfred Primrose for his 'unkind and unfeeling conduct'. The evidence given at the inquest was very damaging to him – apart from being the father of her unborn child, he 'laughed at her, and used some very unkind and undeserving expressions towards her' in the middle of High Street early one Friday afternoon. But did the jury and the Coroner know the full circumstances surrounding Primrose's betrayal of Elizabeth? Records show that the birth of an Alfred Primrose was registered in Sheffield in 1838, the same year as

Elizabeth's death. This certainly wasn't Elizabeth's son as she had died whilst pregnant. Local burial records give an entry for a burial in Sheffield's newly opened General Cemetery. The entry shows that an Alfred Primrose Antcliff, of No.7, Pond Hill, Sheffield, was buried on August 19, 1838, aged just eleven weeks. He had died of a bowel complaint. His parents were Alfred Primrose and Caroline Antcliff who were, significantly, unmarried. From this information there is only one possibility: at the same time that he was seeing Elizabeth Thornhill, Alfred Primrose was also having a relationship with Caroline Antcliff. If the jury had been aware of this fact it is no wonder that they issued such a strong condemnation of Alfred's actions. But there is no mention of this second relationship in the report, so it must be assumed that the jury was not aware of it.

The next intriguing point is the burial record. The informant is not one of baby Alfred's parents but his maternal grandmother Elizabeth Antcliff. This is the last mention of Alfred Primrose senior. The 1841 Census for Sheffield showed his parents Daniel and Martha living at Burgess Street in the town centre, but no sign of Alfred. The same census revealed that Caroline Antcliff was living with her parents John and Elizabeth in Sheaf Row, but again no sign of Alfred. It can only be supposition as to what became of Alfred Primrose. There are two births registered in 1843 in Sheffield for an Alfred Primrose, but these are more likely to be the sons of Alfred senior's brothers, Daniel and Edward. Given his 'activities' and his notoriety after the inquest it is possible that he left Sheffield. Whether he left voluntarily or was 'persuaded' to go may never be known.

Crookesmoor dam, where Elizabeth Thornhill drowned herself

CHAPTER 3

A FATAL CARRIAGE ACCIDENT, LOWER WALKLEY, 1848

'The carriage then struck against the corner of a house, and precipitated all who were in it with fearful violence on to the street'

The 1841 Census records an extensive family living at a large house called Wadsley Park in the Ecclesfield Parish of Sheffield. They were Mark Maugham, aged 51, his wife Grace (46), and children William (19), Mary (12), Matilda (11), Maria (9), Fanny (8) and Henry (3). Also residing there were Samuel Redfern (25), Mary Ann Broomhead (19), Mary Stiving (18) and William Allin (14), probably all domestic servants. The Maughams were clearly a well-to-do family.

However, their world was turned upside down in May 1848. The following report was published in *The Globe* on May 13 of that year.

FATAL ACCIDENT AT SHEFFIELD
An accident occurred at Sheffield on Wednesday morning last, by which Mrs Maugham, the wife of Mr Maugham, a draper of that town, was immediately killed, and by which he received injuries of which he has since died. Mr and Mrs Maugham and their two daughters were driving in a phaeton from their residence, Wadsley Park, when the mare in the shafts became restive, and ran away. It appeared that she was a large mare, and the shafts of the carriage were much too small for her. From

some cause or other, when they arrived part of the way down the hill behind the barracks the horse started off, and the servant ran to the horse's head and tried to stop it, but he could not succeed, and was knocked down; it ran as far as Infirmary Lane, down the Philadelphia Road, when the carriage struck against the corner of a house, and threw them all with terrific violence out of the carriage, which was smashed to pieces. The females were taken into the George the Fourth public house, Mrs Maugham being quite dead at the time, but the two daughters were not seriously injured. Mr Maugham was taken to another inn a little further on, and when laid on a sofa showed signs of life. Medical attendance being procured, he was taken to the infirmary. In the afternoon an inquest was held on the body of Mrs Maugham, and a verdict of accidental death returned. On Wednesday night, at half-past 10 o'clock, Mr Maugham also died of the injuries he had received.

Another report appeared in *The Era* on May 21, 1848. The same account also appeared in *Lloyds Weekly Newspaper*:

FATAL AND DISTRESSING ACCIDENT
Last Wednesday morning, about ten o'clock, Mr and Mrs Maugham, with two of their daughters, left their country residence – a farm called Wadsley Park, Yorkshire – in their four-wheel carriage for their place of business, a drapery shop, in Sheffield. The mare which drew the vehicle had never been put into that carriage before; and in consequence a man servant was employed to run by its side, to render assistance if required. The animal proceeded steadily till it arrived at the bottom of a hill, when, from some unascertained source, it started off at a fearful speed. The servant caught hold of the reins at the mare's head to stop it, but he could not succeed, and in the attempt he was knocked down, after having kept hold for twenty or thirty yards. The carriage then struck against the corner of a house, and precipitated all who were in it with fearful violence on to the street, while the mare broke entirely away, leaving the carriage smashed to pieces. Mrs Maugham was killed on the spot. The daughters, fortunately, did not sustain much injury, the only wound received being a slight cut in Miss Matilda Maugham's head. Mr Maugham was promptly conveyed to the infirmary, apparently in a lifeless state. Mr Maugham recovered his consciousness shortly after he was taken to the infirmary, and the first question he asked related to his wife. An evasive answer was given him, from which he at once concluded that she was dead, and he made no further inquiries on that point. He then sent for Alderman Lowe, and told him that he had not made his will. Mr Maugham dictated, while Mr

Law, of the infirmary, wrote down his wishes as respects the disposal of his property, and completed the document before ten o'clock in the evening, at which time the unfortunate gentleman expired.

To lose both parents was a calamitous event in Victorian England. The children became orphans and unless they were provided for, a grim future beckoned. The deceased couple also had a son, William, who emigrated to New Zealand. His death record reads: 'Oct 31, 1866, near Mangonui, of consumption, Mr William Maugham, son of the late Mark Maugham, draper, of 19 Angel Street, Sheffield, aged 45 years.'

A descendant of William Maugham contacted Chris Hobbs, stating that Mark Maugham, the man who died in the accident, was his great-great-great-grandfather and that he was descended from William, who arrived in New Zealand in 1862. The descendant said: 'Mark Maugham had an estate at Wadsley called Wadsley Park. It was sold by his executors and the site eventually became the Middlewood Hospital, which is now a residential area called Wadsley Park Village. It would appear that the original mansion house no longer exists. After his death he left the drapery shops and the accommodation there to his children. None of them followed William to New Zealand. After William died of tuberculosis in 1866, Sarah, his wife, returned to London to educate the children and then returned to New Zealand where they all settled. She lived to the age of 94 (died 1928) and both Sarah and William are buried together at a place called Peria, which is in the far north of New Zealand, near Mangonui. My father and his siblings recently gained access to the property (now a farm) and restored the grave site.'

CHAPTER 4

TWO GROTESQUE MURDERS AT HEELEY, 1852

'There they found the body of the child ... its head was lying several feet from its body'

In the course of its history, Sheffield has experienced some revolting murders, but the two following crimes are particularly horrific. Even stranger, they occurred within a fortnight of each other, in close proximity, and resulted in the perpetrators being hanged at York Gaol just a week apart. At the time, Heeley, where both bodies were found, was a village outside the boundaries of Sheffield, but was an easy walk or cab ride from the town centre. The first case occurred in August 1852. *The Times* of August 20 described what happened. Those involved lived in the area that today lies directly behind the Midland Station, but the Midland railway did not exist at the time. In the 1850s this area, like much of central Sheffield, was packed with working-class housing.

MURDER.—SHEFFIELD, Aug. 19.—Sheffield is again the scene of one of those horrifying murders which startle a whole country. An illegitimate child, nearly two years old, has had its head cut off by its father, who also attempted to murder its mother and another young woman. The murderer's name is Alfred Waddington, a grinder, residing in Lord-street, Park.

The murderer's name is Alfred Waddington, a grinder, residing in Lord Street, Park. He is about 20 years of age, the associate of notoriously bad characters, and he has himself been tried for highway robbery. The murdered child was called Elizabeth Slater, the daughter of Sarah Slater, of Brown Street, Park, and was about a year and nine months old. On Monday the mother took out a summons, which was to have been heard today, against Waddington, for neglecting to maintain the child. He saw her in the street on Wednesday, and swore he would never pay another farthing towards the support of the child. On Wednesday evening the mother left her child in the care of a little girl called Barlow, and then went to attend the females' evening class at the Mechanics' Institution. About half-past 8 o'clock Waddington appeared at the door of the classroom and called out, 'Sarah Slater, you're wanted.' She went to him, and he asked, 'What have you done with the child?' She told him, and he then said, 'You must go with me; it has fallen off a wall and has broken its neck.' She immediately ran out of the room with him. On arriving in Silvester Lane he said she need not trouble herself for he had murdered the child. He pulled out a large clasp knife and said, 'Here's some of its blood.'

The monster then fiercely attacked her and attempted to cut her throat. She guarded her neck with her hands, which were shockingly lacerated. Waddington was shortly afterwards met by a young woman called Sarah Dobson, who resides in Duke Lane, Sheffield Moor, a companion of the young woman Slater. Having heard rumours of the murder and the attack upon Slater, the young woman asked him what he had done with her and his child. He at once attacked her with his knife, and wounded her severely about the face. Her violent screams caused him to run away. About 2 o'clock this morning, however, he gave himself up to a night watchman, and at the Town Hall he described the exact place where the murdered child might be found. He said he took it from the little girl Barlow, carried it into Cutler's Wood, Heeley, near Sheffield, and there cut its head off. At daylight this morning two policemen went to the place mentioned, and there they found the body of the child. Its head was lying several feet from its body.

The following day a further report appeared in *The Times*:

MURDER AT SHEFFIELD
In The Times *of yesterday an account was given of the horrible murder of a child at Sheffield, by its father, Alfred Waddington, and of an attempt by the murderer to assassinate the mother of the child and*

another young woman. Yesterday the case underwent investigation before Mr T. Badger, the Coroner, and a highly respectable jury, Alfred Waddington, who had given himself up to the police, being present in custody. The body of the murdered child was brought into the room in a basket, and viewed by the coroner and jury. It presented an appalling spectacle. Sarah Slater, the mother of the child, was first examined, and detailed in evidence the circumstances narrated in yesterday's paper. William Jackson, a night constable, stated the circumstances under which he had found the child, with the head severed from the body. Mr Rayner, superintendent of police, detailed to the jury a confession which the prisoner had made to him when in custody. He admitted having murdered the child, but was sorry that he had done so. He said he was much attached to Sarah Slater, but she had taken up with another man, and he wished it had been Sarah rather than the child whose life he had taken. The jury returned a verdict of 'Wilful Murder', and the prisoner was committed to York Castle for trial.

At trial Waddington was found guilty, and was executed on January 8, 1853. He had previous experience of gaol, as the 1851 census shows him as a nineteen-year-old prisoner held in Sheffield. This may have been the occasion he was tried for highway robbery. Prior to his execution Waddington displayed a genuine remorse for his actions and spent his final hours praying in his cell. A crowd of 8,000 gathered to watch him ascend to the scaffold and after muttering, 'Lord Jesus, receive my soul,' he was dispatched by the hangman. His body was buried within the confines of the prison outside the window of the condemned cell.

Cutler's Wood was on the banks of the River Sheaf in the area today called Heeley Bottom. A contemporary writer described the 'lonely walk along Bramall Lane, crossing the River Sheaf by a single plank at Cutler Wood', where highway robberies often occurred. In 1863 the Midland Railway Company obtained the permission of Parliament to compulsorily purchase land on either side of the River Sheaf for the new line from Sheffield to Chesterfield, resulting in the felling of most of the wood. There is still a 'single plank' over the Sheaf in this area in the form of a footbridge that can be reached via a path, known locally as Cutler's Walk, on Queen's Road, then through a foot-tunnel under the railway. The footbridge then leads to a walkway adjacent to the river, along the foot of the towering Skelton's works, and emerges at the Sheaf View public house on Gleadless Road.

The site of the former Cutler's Wood, with its modern-day 'single plank' over the River Sheaf (photograph 2011)

Just a week after the execution of Alfred Waddington, James Barbour, a 21-year-old travelling draper, followed him to the York gallows for the murder, at Heeley, of a former workmate, Alexander Robison, aged 24.

The affair that led to Barbour's hanging began at seven o'clock on the evening of Friday, September 3, 1852, when two boys, George Renton and George Dixon, were picking blackberries on Black Bank, an area that to this day remains an extensive grassy bank, climbing up from East Bank Road towards lower Arbourthorne. There they discovered the body of a man, lying on his front, one hand behind his back, his legs protruding from a hedgerow. The boys ran to raise the alarm at Midhill House (now the Earl Marshal pub), the home of George's grandfather, William Renton, who sent his servant, James Somerset, for help. Soon a policeman arrived on the scene. On examination, the dead man was found to have a serious facial wound, his right-hand trouser pocket turned inside out. There was no money, watch or handkerchief on his person. His only possessions were a pair of lady's scissors and two small song books, in one of which was written the name 'Robison'. The unidentified body was then taken down the hill to the Royal

Standard public house on St Mary's Road. The following morning Inspectors Linley and Tasker found more items near where the dead man had lain, including a silk hat, crushed and pushed into a hedge, a white silk handkerchief covered in dried blood, and a bottle of laudanum. Five or six yards away from where the body was found there was a pool of blood, covered over with loose grass, and the surrounding ground was trodden down, as if a violent scuffle had taken place there. The police released a description of the man: he was 5' 9" in height, of stout, muscular build and had sandy hair and moustache. His clothes were of good quality, comprising a jacket, black waistcoat, fine cotton shirt, tweed trousers and wellington boots.

Black Bank, where the body was found. East Bank Road is to the left, Midhill House (now the Earl Marshal pub) behind the trees (photograph 2010)

Still with no idea as to the man's identity, an inquest was opened by the Deputy Coroner, Mr Joseph Badger, at the Royal Standard on Saturday afternoon. However, a clue had been found in the man's clothing; very faintly, the name 'A. Robison'. The police surgeon, Mr R. Roper, assisted by Mr H. Payne, undertook a post-mortem examination of the body. Roper informed the inquest that he found a circular cut at the crown of the back of the head, into which a finger might be introduced two inches. Behind the right ear there was another circular wound, passing obliquely upwards and forwards. On the right side of the face were four cleanly incised wounds, extending down and across the face and under the jaw. Behind the right ear was a discolouration that might have been caused by an explosion of gunpowder in close proximity. The lower jaw was fractured on the right side, and at the front there was a clean fracture, as if done by a violent and heavy blow. On opening the skull there was found in the brain, in the wound at the back of the head, some gun wadding, several flattened No.4 shot, and some bone fragments. Some No.4 shot, not flattened, were also found in the wound in the brain at the back of the right ear. The orbit of the eye and the bones of the nose were fractured. In the stomach was found a quantity of undigested food, which appeared to be duck and onions, consumed, in Mr Roper's opinion, not more than two or three hours before death. There was no doubt that the head wounds were the cause of death, and it was probable that the victim had been shot from behind. It was impossible for him to have inflicted the wounds upon himself.

That morning the *Sheffield Times* had reported that the body was that of a man called Scrimshaw who had committed suicide. However, Scrimshaw had since turned up alive. On Saturday afternoon a young Scotsman named M'Donald, who was reported by *The Times* of London to be 'connected with one of the Sheffield newspapers', having read about the name being found in the man's clothing and believing that he was dressed in the manner of a Scottish packman, requested to view the body. He identified the deceased as Alexander Robison, a draper, of Doncaster, employed by Mr David Barbour. The employer was sent for, and he confirmed it was Robison, a 24-year-old native of Dumfriesshire. Barbour said he was 'a very stout, tall young man, well able to fight two men if he had a fair chance'. Robison had been in his employ for well over three years as a travelling packman. He had left Doncaster on Monday, August 30, with a pack containing a quantity of linen goods, and a silver watch and guard, given to him by Barbour. His duty was to travel round Sheffield, sell the goods, collect the takings and return to Doncaster on Thursday night. It was expected that he would have collected about six or seven pounds, but he did not return to Doncaster that Thursday.

The landlord of the Royal Standard informed the police that the day before the discovery of the body a customer had handed him a pack for safe keeping before ordering a cab to take him to the Reindeer public house in the town centre. This person had seemed uneasy and flustered. The landlord gave the pack to Inspector Linley, who found specks of blood on it. At this point the inquest was adjourned, to be reconvened at the Town Hall the following Wednesday.

The Royal Standard public house, where the body was taken and the inquest opened (photograph 2010)

Further police enquiries revealed that Robison had been lodging at a public house, Naylor's, on Watson's Walk, between Angel Street and Hartshead in the town centre. He often stayed there before returning by train to Doncaster. The landlord, George Naylor, knew Robison well and told police that his regular lodger owned a silver watch and chain, which were missing when his body was found. Naylor said that on Thursday, September 2, Robison had lunched at Gray's restaurant, also on Watson's Walk, with three friends – James Barbour, cousin of Robison's employer David Barbour, James Fagan and Finman M'Clelland. The latter two were also Scotsmen, both travelling drapers, whilst Barbour also used to work for his cousin. They then returned to Naylor's for a drink. There, Barbour told the men that he was going to introduce Robison to some potential new customers. Tellingly, Naylor stated that Robison was carrying a pack. Soon afterwards, at about two o'clock, Fagan and M'Clelland left the party. M'Clelland informed the resumed inquest that that was the last time he saw Robison alive.

Another witness, George M'Cormick, supplied vital information. M'Cormick, who worked for James Barbour, testified that he shared lodgings with him at No.105 New Meadow Street, Netherthorpe. M'Cormick noticed that Barbour had in his possession a silver watch that he had not seen before. On Saturday

Barbour asked M'Cormick to pawn the watch for him at Mr W. C. Beet's West Street pawnbroker's shop, but in the name of William Smith, not James Barbour. M'Cormick obtained thirty shillings for the watch, which he handed over to Barbour, along with the pawn ticket, at the Reindeer public house on Devonshire Street. He then said that as the hours passed Barbour appeared more and more worried about something. Next David Barbour was called to give evidence. He stated that he had given a silver watch and guard to Robison. Initially he had been going to give the watch to his cousin James, whom he once employed, until he had cause to dismiss him for embezzlement. David Barbour was now suspicious of his cousin's actions, and had passed on his suspicions to the police. The following Sunday James Barbour was interviewed by police but not arrested. He admitted to dining with Robison the day before his body was discovered, but claimed the men then parted, and he believed Robison was on his way to catch a train to Doncaster, as he usually did on a Thursday afternoon.

The next morning, however, David Barbour informed the police of the serial number of the watch he had presented to Robison. Upon receipt of this information police made visits to a number of pawnshops in town, the watch soon being found at Beet's. A warrant for James Barbour's arrest was issued. Inspector Astwood and Detective Officer Silk carried out the arrest and in order to convey Barbour to the Town Hall, where he was to be formally charged, they took a cab. By chance the cab driver was the same one who took the fare from the Royal Standard to the Reindeer on that fateful Thursday, and he recognised Barbour as his customer. The flustered man who left the pack with the landlord of the Royal Standard was therefore presumed to be James Barbour.

At the Town Hall the Superintendent, Thomas Rayner, charged Barbour with the wilful murder of Alexander Robison; Barbour denied having any part in it. Sarah Jane Beet, sister of the West Street pawnbroker, could not identify Barbour but pointed out George M'Cormick as the man who pawned the watch. Both men were remanded in custody, but M'Cormick was later brought as a witness against Barbour. With this new evidence at hand, the inquest jury returned a verdict of wilful murder against James Barbour, and the Coroner committed him for trial at York Assizes. The trial commenced on December 21, 1852 and was reported in detail by *The Times* on December 24:

WINTER ASSIZES.

YORK, DEC. 21.
EXTRAORDINARY CASE.
CROWN COURT.—(*Before Mr. Justice* TALFOURD.)

James Barbour, aged 21, was indicted for the wilful murder of Alexander Robison at Sheffield, on the 2d of September last.

Mr. Overend, Mr. Pickering, and Mr. Johnstone appeared for the prosecution; and Mr. Serjeant Wilkins (specially retained) and Mr. Hardy for the prisoner.

Mr Overend stated the facts of the case to the jury with great clearness and ability. The question then arose, by whom had [Robison] been murdered? The prisoner at the bar was a cousin of Mr [David] Barbour, of Doncaster, and had formerly been employed by him in the same manner and to travel in the same district as the deceased, taking the money obtained for his goods back to his master. The man had been dismissed in August last by Mr Barbour. The prisoner and the deceased had both been in Mr Barbour's employ at the same time, and were companions and slept in the same bed. The prisoner, after he was dismissed, was absent in Scotland about a fortnight, and then returned to Sheffield, and had been there only a very short time indeed before this occurrence happened. He employed a young man named M'Cormick, and the prisoner and M'Cormick lodged in Sheffield with a person named Pigot

On Thursday, the 2nd of September, the last day that the deceased was seen alive, the prisoner, the deceased, and two other Scotchmen, named M'Clelland and Fagan, were in company together in Sheffield, and dined together at 1 o'clock at an eating-house on roast duck stuffed with onions. The prisoner then stated that he was about to leave Sheffield for London. At half-past 1 they all adjourned to Naylor's public house, where they had some porter. At that time the deceased was wearing his silver watch and silver guard, and he also had with him a pack of drapery goods. They then left Naylor's, M'Clelland asking the prisoner and the deceased where they were going. The prisoner replied he was going to show Robison some customers that Barbour knew nothing of, and after that he should go to London and the south in a day or two, as he thought the south was better for business. They left Naylor's about 2 o'clock and parted at the bottom of

31

Watson's Walk, M'Clelland and Fagan going one way, and the prisoner and the deceased another.

For an hour after that there was no evidence of what had become of them; but at 3 o'clock an old man by the name of George Hind was seated on a stile leading to a footpath crossing some fields in the outskirts of Sheffield, and 640 yards from the place where the body was found, when two men came up to the stile from the direction of Sheffield. One was a taller man than the other and carried a bundle under his arm. Hind said to them, as they came up to the stile to get over it, 'I will give you room, gentlemen,' and they got over into the field. The smaller man, as he was passing him, said, 'What are you doing here? You should have some employment.' Hind answered, 'I have as much right to be here smoking a whiff of tobacco as you have.' The smaller of the two men called out to the other, 'Let this man bring one of your bundles.' The man who so spoke to George Hind, Hind identified as the prisoner, and the taller man was the deceased. A man named Christopher Corbett, coming from Newfield Green to Sheffield by the footpath across the fields, which is very little frequented, met two men going towards Newfield Green, one taller than the other, and carrying a pack. The prisoner was the shorter man of the two; the taller one answered the description of the deceased. This was between 3 and 4 o'clock, and 375 yards from the place where the body was afterwards found. About that time a young man named Charles Renton was in a field adjoining to that in which the body was found when he heard two shots fired quickly after each other. He was lying down in the next field, about 200 yards from the place where the body was. The field in which the body was found was a grass field, having no pathway across it. Why the prisoner and the deceased had entered that field was not known.

The prisoner was expected back at Naylor's at 5, but never returned. About 4 o'clock that afternoon the prisoner entered the Royal Standard public house. He was then alone, appeared heated, as if from walking very fast, and was carrying a pack. When last seen he had no pack, but the deceased had; when the deceased's body was found there was no pack. He asked the landlord, who was a stranger to him, to take charge of his pack, and said that he would call for it on the following morning. The prisoner never did call for it. This pack was shown to be the pack of the deceased, and Mr [David] Barbour identified his private marks on some of the drapery goods it contained. The landlord placed the pack in a closet and locked it up, and next day, when some enquiry was made as to the dead body which had been found, he delivered up the *pack to the police. While at the Royal Standard the prisoner wanted a cab. He also asked for a brush, to brush the mud from his shoes and the bottom of his trousers, as they were covered with mud and clay. Between the field where the body was found and the Royal Standard public house were a number of ploughed fields of clay soil, across which the prisoner might have come if he had wished to avoid the public road; and, had he done so, in all probability his shoes and clothes would be so marked. The cab came up, and he immediately drove away to a public house in Sheffield but a short distance off, and it was a matter of observation that a man in the prisoner's condition should be taking a cab for a short distance from one public house to another. The prisoner drove to the Reindeer, where he found M'Cormick. He stayed there a short time, and went to his lodgings about a quarter to 6 o'clock. Mr Pigot was there, and one or two other persons. One of them asked what time it was, when the prisoner pulled a silver watch and guard out of his breeches pocket. Pigot said, 'Hallo, you have got a watch, Mr Barbour,' he not having had one before. The prisoner answered, 'Yes, I had sold it some time since, but not having got paid for it I took it back.' About 11 o'clock he went to bed. The prisoner pulled out the watch and laid it on the dressing table, and M'Cormick asked him, 'How did you get this?' The prisoner replied, 'Oh, I had it in a pledge, but did not like to tell about it.'*

Next day, a man, believed to be the prisoner, pawned a pistol at a pawnbroker's in Sheffield. On that day he told M'Cormick that he wished to sell some debts for 30 pounds that he had to collect. That night Pigot observed that the prisoner had not his watch, and asked him what he had done with it, and he said 'it had happened in an accident' and he had sent it to the watchmaker. On Saturday, the morning after, he asked M'Cormick to meet him at the Reindeer and pawn his watch for him. M'Cormick did so, and gave the ticket to the prisoner. On the Monday after the prisoner was taken into custody, and on his person the pawn ticket for the watch was found. When asked about the pawn ticket he said he had bought it from a man in West Street. That watch was identified by Mr Barbour, of Doncaster, as the one worn by the deceased, and which he had given to him. On the Saturday after the murder, while sitting in his lodgings, a daughter of Mr Pigot said, 'There has been a murder in Sheffield, and the body is lying at the Royal Standard.' Pigot said he should go and see it, and asked the prisoner to go with him. The prisoner declined, saying 'he did not like to see such sights'. When Pigot got home he expressed great anxiety to know about the murdered man, and was told that 'Robison' was marked on the linen on the body. The prisoner then said he knew a little of him when he lived at Doncaster, and it was a pity he had come to an untimely end. Pigot did not see the body that night, as it was locked up, and the prisoner wished him very much to go and see it next morning, but refused to go with him. At this time the body had not been identified. When Pigot returned, he asked how the body looked, and how it was found; and when Pigot said that a bottle of laudanum had been found near it, he asked 'if a coroner's jury would find that he made away with himself?' He then said he thought there must be some woman in it.

On Sunday he met Police Officer Aston in the street, and began talking about the deceased to him, saying his death was a 'mysterious affair' and he then told Aston that the deceased was last seen in a cab at half-past 6 o'clock on Thursday night, with a Doncaster woman, at the Reindeer public house. Mrs Swann, the landlady, proved this to be untrue. Mr Rayner, a police officer, of Sheffield, having heard that the body was identified, and that the prisoner had been seen in the deceased's company, sent to the prisoner on Saturday to ask him what he knew of the deceased. He described correctly where they had dined together, and said that after that he parted from the deceased in Watson's Walk, when the deceased said he was going to Doncaster at 6 o'clock. The prisoner, on returning home after this, told Pigot that he had been giving evidence to Mr Rayner, about the deceased, and he then said, 'Poor fellow! We were the best of friends; we ate and drank and slept together.' Pigot said, 'Why, you said this morning you only knew him slightly?' The prisoner appeared to be much confused, threw his head back, and said, 'he was in an awful state of mind, owing to M'Cormick being out, and being alone.' On Monday, about 2 o'clock, the prisoner went to the Reindeer and saw Mrs Swann, the landlady. She said to him, 'What a shocking thing about this poor young man; have you seen the body?' The prisoner answered, 'No, I would not see it for 50 pounds.' 'Why,' she said, 'you were his companion?' The prisoner said, 'He knew it on Friday night.' She replied, 'It is very queer you did not mention it here on Saturday, and that you did not go to the funeral.'

Mr Rayner hearing these stories about the prisoner caused him to be apprehended, and upon him were found 2 pounds 15 shillings in money, and a receipt for a post-office registered letter, bearing the date September 3, for 2 pounds, addressed to Mr John Barbour, Bowness, *near Carlisle. He was at this time out of employment, and had received no money from M'Cormick. He also told Mr Rayner that the deceased Robison had given him his pack to take care of when he parted from him. Mrs Swann, on being recalled, stated that she had changed the prisoner two sovereigns for 2 pounds' worth of silver on Friday, the 3rd of September, which she saw him place into a slit card and enclose in a letter. The clothes of the murdered man were produced, and this closed the case for the prosecution.*

DEC. 22
This morning the trial of James Barbour was resumed at 9 o'clock. Mr Serjeant Wilkins proceeded to address the jury for the defence. He implored them to banish all prejudice from their minds, and to consider the facts of the case with impartiality like reasoning men. The evidence was entirely circumstantial. What motive was there for the prisoner to commit the crime imputed to him? He and the deceased were friends and companions, and the prisoner was showing him good offices on the very day of the murder. It was suggested that robbery was the motive. But the little money the deceased had upon him could be no inducement to the prisoner for the commission of such a crime, because he was not without means. It was easy for him to have obliterated the private marks from the drapery goods in the pack if his object was to steal them. It was suggested that Hind and Corbett might be mistaken as to the prisoner's identity when passing through the fields with the deceased. If not mistaken, he contended it was impossible for the prisoner to have induced the deceased to leave the footpath 370 yards, to have committed the murder, and to have got back to the Royal Standard public house by 4 o'clock. Corbett speaking of the time when he met the prisoner and the deceased being half-past 3, and it was in evidence that it took 25 minutes to walk quickly from the place where the body was found to the Royal Standard inn. For what purpose had the deceased gone into the field? The prisoner had said, 'He thought there was a woman in the case.' The song books found on the deceased contained immoral songs. The man who carried such books in his pocket would be capable of other immoralities, and he suggested that what the prisoner had said, that 'the deceased had given him the pack to take care of for him', was true, as it was also with regard to the watch, while the deceased crossed from the pathway into the field with some woman for an immoral purpose. The state of the ground where the body was found showed that a violent struggle had taken place. Was it likely that the prisoner alone – he not having a scratch or a spot of

blood on him – could have been engaged in that struggle, the evidence being that the deceased 'was able to do for two such as him'? He suggested that in attendance upon the woman there had been men lurking near ready to commit violence, and that the murder had been committed by more than one man. The learned counsel then went through the evidence with great skill and power, and implored the jury not to be led to a conclusion that the prisoner was guilty by facts which, he submitted, were not conclusive.

His Lordship then proceeded to sum up the evidence. He thought it right to admonish the jury against being led by the very powerful address they had just heard to do injustice. They were to find their verdict according to the evidence; and his advice to them was to do their duty fearing God, and to have regard to the consequences. The jury retired, and after an absence of a quarter of an hour returned with a verdict of Guilty. The usual proclamation having been made, and the prisoner having been called upon to say why sentence of death should not be passed upon him, his Lordship, having put on the black cap, proceeded to pass on him the dreadful sentence of the law. He said, the prisoner had had the advantage of being defended with unrivalled ability, but the decision to which the jury had arrived had his entire concurrence. The prisoner had been found guilty of a most savage and barbarous murder, unexampled in his experience. In the midst of youth and health and thoughtlessness he had suddenly and treacherously taken the life of his companion. To the prisoner the law would be more merciful than he had been to his friend. Opportunity for prayer and repentance would be afforded to him; and he implored him to avail himself, during the few days he had yet to live, of the religious consolation which would be provided for him. His Lordship then passed the awful sentence in the usual form.

The prisoner, who throughout the trial had preserved a sullen unmoved expression, except by a slight paleness which overspread his face on hearing the verdict, showed no symptom of feeling whatever. Immediately after his Lordship had concluded passing sentence he said, 'Thank you, my Lord, I am innocent.'

An appeal against the conviction was made to the Home Secretary, Lord Palmerston. All the while Barbour claimed that he was innocent and that George M'Cormick was the man responsible for killing Robison. The appeal delayed his scheduled execution by one week, but it did no good. Shortly before being led to the gallows, Barbour finally admitted he had murdered

Robison, and absolved M'Cormick of any involvement. At noon on January 15, 1853, exactly one week after the execution of Alfred Waddington for an equally dastardly murder committed less than a mile from where Barbour's crime took place, James Barbour was hanged from the same gallows. Despite heavy rain, four thousand people witnessed the bolt being drawn, though it took a while as the executioner, an old man, had difficulty doing so and needed assistance. Barbour shouted, 'Lord, have mercy on my soul' as he awaited his fate. His body was left hanging for an hour before being buried in the same grave as Alfred Waddington.

And so ended a particularly gruesome few months in the history of Sheffield, and especially Heeley. Two awful murders so close together in both time and location, followed by two murder trials and two hangings, separated by one week, at the same prison. It was somehow appropriate that two such wretches should face the final humiliation of sharing a grave.

CHAPTER 5

A BOY BURNT TO DEATH, HEELEY, 1852

'The child ran nearly three quarters of a mile enveloped in his burning clothes'

On October 2, 1852, the *Sheffield and Rotherham Independent* reported:

SHOCKING DEATH OF A BOY AT UPPER HEELEY.—
An inquest was held before Thomas Badger, Esq., at the Bull Inn,
Upper Heeley, on Saturday last, on the body of George Memmott,
aged 4 years, son of John Memmott, cutler, Common side, Upper
Heeley, who died on the evening of the preceding day, from injuries
received by being burnt.

On Friday afternoon, the deceased and a boy named John Fish were amusing themselves in a field of Mr Appleyard, the Ash farm, Upper Heeley, and which adjoins that in which Robinson was murdered a few weeks ago. There was a fire in the field to consume the litter, and the children employed themselves in carrying 'twitch' to feed it with. Whilst doing this the clothes of the deceased caught fire, and he immediately started home in great alarm. The child ran nearly three quarters of a mile enveloped in his burning clothes, but, when within a few hundred yards of home, he sank down exhausted in a field. The little sufferer was carried home, and Mr Taylor, surgeon, sent for, but the child was beyond the reach of help, and died the same evening. His body was blackened by the fire, and the place where he had lain in the field was distinctly perceptible from its scorched appearance. It appears that there was a man in the field where the accident occurred at the time when it happened, but he did not see it, as the deceased made no alarm, but as soon as his pinafore had taken fire hastened off in the direction of home.

Ash Farm was situated above the Ball Inn at the top of Myrtle Road. It was demolished only when the building of new houses on the former Ball Inn recreation ground (Sheffield United's old training ground) was commenced in the mid-2000s, having stood derelict for many years. Common side, where the boy lived, was probably the area known today as Gleadless Common, which ties in with the report as it is about a mile away from the site of Ash Farm. The murder of 'Robinson' mentioned in the report is covered in the previous chapter. In that chapter he was named as 'Robison' but some reports referred to him as 'Robinson'.

The site of Ash Farm, Upper Heeley, now covered by new houses. The Ball Inn is beyond the houses (photograph 2012)

CHAPTER 6

FATAL ASSAULT AT THE OWLERTON FEAST, 1854

'He was struck repeatedly on the head by first one and then another'

The Era newspaper of July 23, 1854 gave the following account of a terrible incident near Sheffield:

> BRUTAL MURDER AT OWLERTON, NEAR SHEFFIELD.—
> A cowardly outrage, committed at Owlerton, on the 4th July, has re-
> sulted in the death of the victim, Joseph Crookes, jun., saw grinder,
> Hill-bridge.

The offence was committed at the Owlerton Feast where the murdered man went on the night of Monday, 3rd July and stayed drinking at the Sportsman Groom public house till about two in the morning. During the night a quarrel had taken place between Crookes and one or two of the men in the room and when the company all left the house at the request of the landlord, five or six of the men – two of them with heavy sticks and another with a thick sharpened log of wood – waited outside the door and upon Crookes coming out, commenced a brutal attack upon him, in the course of which they inflicted such injuries as ultimately resulted in his death. All the parties, including the murdered man, were more or less intoxicated. The names of the persons implicated were John Ashmore, table blade forger, Charles Carpenter, and Henry Thompson. They have been brought before Mr Sorby, the

40

Coroner, and the jury after a long investigation returned a verdict of wilful murder.

The report mentions the Sportsman Groom public house. This is incorrect; there was for many years a Sportsman Group public house on the corner of Penistone Road and Owlerton Green, but was demolished as part of a road-widening scheme. Douglas Lamb's book *A Pub On Every Corner* states that the Sportsman Group stood at No.851 Penistone Road, was built in 1833 and knocked down in 1989. The Swann Morton company now stands on the site. The Owlerton area was still essentially rural in the mid nineteenth century, as this postcard, from fifty years later, shows:

The brief account above was expanded upon by a report of the subsequent court case in *The Times*. Some confusion arises here as the alleged assailants were named in the first report as John Ashmore, Charles Carpenter and Henry Thompson, but *The Times* named them differently, also adding a fourth man to those charged.

WINTER ASSIZES - NORTHERN CIRCUIT - YORK, DEC 7
Crown Court (Before Mr Baron Alderson)
John Holroyd, Charles Haines, George Knowles, and Joseph Peech, were indicted for the wilful murder of Joseph Crookes, at Ecclesfield, near Sheffield, on the 4th of July last. Mr Dearsley, and Mr Johnston prosecuted; Mr Heaton defended the prisoner Holroyd, Mr Campbell Foster Haines, Mr D. Seymour Knowles, and Mr Overend, the prisoner Peech.

It appeared that on the 4th of July last, it being the village feast of Owlerton, the deceased went to the Sportsman Groom public house, kept by a man named Hollins, at which there was a dance. The deceased went there about 6 o'clock in the evening, left, and again returned about midnight. About that time the four prisoners and a number of other men from Sheffield appeared also to have gone to the house and engaged in the dancing going on. The deceased was the worse for liquor, and so conducted himself as to give offence to several of the Sheffield men; and about 2 o'clock in the morning he was challenged to fight, and engaged in a scuffle with two or three of the prisoners, and received a bloody nose in the dancing room in the fray. It appeared also that he had endeavoured to make peace with the men with whom he had been fighting by treating them to drink. In the midst of one of the scuffles the landlord entered the room and told them they must all leave, and cleared the house. At that time there were upwards of 20 people, chiefly men, and some women.

The prisoners, who all came from Sheffield, left together, and the deceased in a minute or two followed after them. Immediately on the deceased leaving the house, and getting into the road, according to some of the witnesses, the prisoners pulled him down on the road, and according to others, struck him down with a cart-cotter. These men were said to be of the Sheffield party. Some of the witnesses said Holroyd was the man who struck the deceased the first blow with a gutta-percha stick; according to others Knowles was the first man who struck him, and knocked him down with a cart-prop; while another witness said Haines first knocked him down. When down he was struck repeatedly on the head by first one and then another with the cart-prop, a piece of wood a yard and a half long and as thick as a man's wrist, with a cart-cotter, and with a piece of wood three inches square, and of some length, which had been obtained from a cart near. A man named Ashmore was also seen to strike the deceased a swinging blow with the cart-cotter, as also a man named Sykes; and Peech was spoken to by one witness as having struck him on the head with the square piece of timber. Haines was said to be like Ashmore in appearance, and the witnesses differed as to which of them got the cart-cotter from the cart. It was dusk at the time – between light and dark. A man named Rutherford came to the door to endeavour to make peace, and while standing there stones and oyster-shells were thrown at him and he went in again. He returned again, and while talking to two of the men was struck by a third. He went into the house for the poker, with which he armed himself and returned, and struck about with the poker, the deceased at the time being on the ground, and all the prisoners, except

Peech, described as striking him repeatedly with first one and then another of the weapons with which they had armed themselves from the cart.

At length the landlord came out armed with his gun, and threatened to shoot among them if they did not go away. The men then all went away, and the deceased was found insensible and bleeding from two serious wounds on his head. He was carried into the house and washed, and afterwards assisted home, and a surgeon called in immediately to attend him. The surgeon, Mr Moore, of Sheffield, stated that he found the deceased bleeding from his nose, mouth, and left ear, and vomiting blood mixed with liquor. He had several bruises about his head, face and shoulders. He had a wound two inches long, cut to the bone, on the top of his head, and a little further back was a tumour. The man died on the 5th of July, and the surgeon made a post-mortem examination of his head. The tumour was found full of bloody pus, and on taking off the scalp he found an extensive fracture of the parietal and temporal bones, extending half round the head, and immediately beneath the two wounds. A piece of bone had been driven out of the temporal bone. The fracture was the primary cause of death. One of these wounds must have been made with an edged, the other with a blunt, instrument. There was abundant evidence to show that all the prisoners, except Peech, who was only spoken to by one witness, had struck the deceased with one or other of the weapons after he was on the ground.

The defence on behalf of each prisoner was that the circumstances, as proved, could not amount to more than manslaughter, supposing that the evidence given in support of the charge was fully believed, and much ingenuity was displayed in endeavouring, on the part of each of the counsel, to remove from the shoulders of their own individual clients the culpability of the transactions and they all urged that at the time of the morning, in the midst of a drunken squabble at a village feast, it was impossible to say whose hand struck the fatal blow, and how far the deceased had brought the attack upon himself, which it was contended was without concert. His Lordship, in summing up most carefully, directed the jury as to the law, and what would constitute murder. If the act of killing were done with an intention to kill, and was neither justifiable in point of law nor excusable from prior provocation, it was murder. If a man beat another with a deadly weapon so as to cause death, it was murder, as his intention must be presumed from the kind of weapon used. But a weapon might be used which might either be intended to kill or merely to beat a man. If, in that case, with such a *weapon, a man beat another to such excess as to put his life in danger, the jury might infer from that an intention to kill, which was necessary to constitute the first step in murder. There was another complication. If the blows were all struck by one man, he must know of the excess, and his intention to kill must be inferred from that knowledge, and that would be murder. But when the excess arose from a great number of isolated acts by different men, they could not put all those acts together so as to constitute the excess of violence which allowed an intention to kill, unless they brought knowledge of all the blows to each man. But if, seeing a man beaten several blows, a man went and struck the last blow, that last blow might constitute the excess of violence which caused death, and that man was responsible for all the blows. The question here was, was the excess of blows brought home to the knowledge of the prisoner?*

His Lordship then alluded to the want of light, and the possibility of the prisoners not being able to see the effect of the blows. No proof at all had been given by whom the blows had been struck that had caused the death, and the weapons which might have inflicted the blows had been used by all the prisoners. But if in the course of the scuffle many blows were given, had those engaged in it a common purpose in inflicting them? If they had, and they could not be aware of the excess, the killing would be manslaughter; if aware of the excess it would be murder. His Lordship then called attention to the prisoners all setting upon the deceased the moment he appeared outside the house, as evidencing a common purpose to beat him. Probably they were filled with resentment at having been turned out of the house, and at having had their festivity broken up by the conduct of the deceased in the dancing room. Their having hastily picked up weapons from a cart showed they were unprepared to inflict injury on the deceased, and pointed to the nature of the offence being rather that of manslaughter than murder. His Lordship then read the evidence. If the evidence satisfied them that all the prisoners except Peech took part in the excess of violence knowing it to be excess, it would be murder; it they all took part in it not knowing it to be excess, it would be manslaughter. If they were not satisfied that all or any of them took part in the violence, they or he must be acquitted. The jury retired, and, after an absence of half an hour, returned with a verdict of Guilty of manslaughter against all except Peech, who was acquitted by direction of his Lordship. The case occupied nearly all day. Sentence was deferred.

The deferral of sentence lasted just one day. On December 8, 1854 The *Leeds Mercury* reported Mr Baron Alderson's judgement on the three defendants. The report stated:

> *John Holroyd, Charles Haines and George Knowles, convicted of manslaughter at Owlerton, near Sheffield, last July, were severely sentenced to six years' penal servitude. In passing sentence upon the prisoners, the learned judge said that the jury had very properly found the prisoners guilty of manslaughter, a crime that was committed under circumstances of considerable violence, they being at the same time more or less intoxicated. It seems that six or seven of them had attacked the deceased with weapons which most certainly they had seized in a hasty manner – still the attack was cruel, cowardly and unlawful – cowardly because there were some seven to one – cruel because their weapons were heavy and improper – and unlawful because they had committed an outrage against society. He must therefore punish them with severity. He had hesitated whether he ought not to transport then for a long term of years, but he should not send them out of the country. The sentence of the court was that they each undergo six years' penal servitude.*

It is interesting to note that one of the options open to the judge was to send the men to Australia! It is difficult in hindsight to get the 'feel' of a case such as this but the impression is that the defendants were treated rather leniently. By the 1850s transportation to Australia was in its final throes and it was possibly this factor that mitigated the sentence. If the death had occurred thirty years earlier the three defendants would definitely have been transported. They were also fortunate that the case at the Winter Assizes came before Mr Baron Alderson, who, by the standards of the Victorian era, was a more thoughtful and merciful judge than many others.

But perhaps the most fascinating aspect of the whole event is the modern parallel. Crowds of men shouting, drunk, fighting and assaulting each other in the street; you could almost think it was Sheffield in the 21st century, but it was over 150 years ago. The traditions of the Owlerton Feast live on!

CHAPTER 7

THE DEATH OF A SHEFFIELD POLICEMAN, 1855

'*Beardshaw put his hand to his head and said, "Oh, my head!"*'

The first death of a policeman in Sheffield occurred on July 22, 1855. The term 'policeman' in this context is rather a misnomer, as policing the towns in the middle of the nineteenth century was far removed from modern-day policing, as explained in the following extract from the website *www.historyandpolicy.org*:

The 1835 Municipal Corporations Act introduced ratepayer democracy to the several hundred self-governing towns of England and Wales. The only compulsory statutory duty of the newly elected councils was to select a watch committee from their number to run the police force. In this self-confident, prosperous, and autonomous urban world, most boroughs introduced uniformed 'new' police forces, or took over existing (often very efficient) forces. The committees had complete power over the activities and composition of their forces. This reform in the towns was matched by rural areas through the introduction of the county police in 1839-40, through acts which gave counties the power to introduce police forces. Policing power was largely exercised by local government, and the boroughs of England and Wales fiercely protected the police powers exercised by their elected watch committees. These powers were symbolic of the city's independence, and police forces were crucial exercisers of executive power locally.

William Beardshaw, the unfortunate man killed, is better described as a 'watchman' rather than a 'policeman' and many newspaper reports of the period referred to 'watchmen'. The details of the incident are related in the *Daily News* report of the York Winter Assizes of December 12, 1855, before Mr Baron Martin. Note that – if they are the same men – in this instance Mr Dearsley defended, whereas the previous year he prosecuted the 'Owlerton Feast' case, whilst Mr Johnston prosecuted on both occasions.

JAMES BURKE, 22, and CORMACK DUNLEVY, 32, were indicted for the murder of Wm. Beardshaw, at Sheffield, on the 22nd of July last.

Mr. HARDY and Mr. JOHNSTON conducted the prosecution; the prisoners were defended by Mr. DEARSLEY.

Mr Hardy briefly stated the case. The person who came by his death on the 22nd of July, by the hand of someone, was a man named Beardshaw, who was acting on that day for the first time as a watchman in the town of Sheffield. It appeared that a man named McCormack was supposed to have been committing a robbery in the shop of John Shannan, who charged him with the offence. McCormack escaped but was shortly afterwards apprehended in the neighbourhood by a policeman and irons were put on his hands and legs in consequence of his violent conduct. About a thousand of McCormack's fellow countrymen (Irishmen) were assembled near the place where he (McCormack) was apprehended and on the policemen attempting to put him in the cab, for the purpose of conveying him to the police station, he called out to the Irishmen, 'Will you see me taken?' or words to that effect. Immediately upon this, an attack was made on the police, stones and brickbats being thrown by the mob, and McCormack was rescued, but apprehended at a later period in the evening, when it was discovered that he had employed the time which had intervened from his rescue in removing the irons which the police had put upon him. In the course of the melee Beardshaw received the injuries which caused his death and another policeman named Dickinson was also severely injured. The deceased was at the time in the execution of his duty, taking into custody a man charged with a serious offence and if the prisoners were two of the parties who attempted to rescue this man by violence they must be considered responsible for the effects produced by such means as they employed. It would be proved that the prisoners were extremely violent; they were seen by many witnesses to throw stones and use other violence to the police. This was not the case of a private disturbance between individuals; here were police officers in the execution of their duty, and he (the learned counsel) should submit under the correction of his Lordship, that anything that was done to them resulting in death would bring the offence within the crime of murder. Mr Baron Martin dissented from this view of the law; to convict of murder the intention must be brought home to the person committing the crime. Mr Hardy said that after this intimation from the learned judge, he would abandon the capital offence, and charge the prisoners with the manslaughter of Beardshaw, merely.

The witnesses for the prosecution were called. Amongst these – Jane Jubb, deposed that on the night in question she saw Burke throw a stone in the melee and on a companion saying to him, 'Get out of the way, you have hurt a watchman,' he exclaimed with an oath that he would kill the watchman – Geo Rushton, a police constable, proved that he saw Dunlevy throw stones twice at the police; he was twice hit – John Hill also saw Burke throw stones and heard him say that he would 'kill the --------- watchman'. He was assisting in conveying Dickinson, who had been injured, to the infirmary when Burke struck him (witness) over the back with a stone in a stocking, and he also stabbed him in the right arm with a knife – Thomas Chapsey, proved that Burke kicked two policemen who had been knocked down in a gutter – Samson Barker, police constable, deposed that when McCormack was being put into the cab, he and Beardshaw were knocked down. Beardshaw put his hand to his head and said, 'Oh, my head!' – Samuel Lindley saw the riot. Both the prisoners were present and they appeared to take a very active part in the disturbance – Mr Wright, surgeon, proved that the deceased's skull was fractured, and the consequent extravation of blood on the brain was the cause of death. The wound was such a one as was likely to have been produced by a stone.

Mr Dearsley, on rising to address the jury for the defence, remarked that he would yield to no man in struggling to the last for a client when there was anything like a fair chance of success; but when there was not he would not do it to please any client. The question was, were the jury satisfied that the witnesses who had spoken to the prisoners throwing the stones and striking persons were to be believed. He had no instructions that he could shake their credibility and without such instructions it would be improper for him to do so. Therefore all he could say was this; the night was dark, there was no light, and it was *within the range of possibility, and that was all, that some of the witnesses may have been mistaken. Mr Baron Martin told the jury that there was no evidence of murder at all, and the jury found the prisoners guilty of manslaughter.*

The same newspaper then proceeded to outline a further case against four other persons that arose out of the same incident:

RIOT AT SHEFFIELD
William McCormack, 32, Patrick Charleston, 19, Michael Finnerty, 46, and Robert Smith, 38, were indicted for a riot at Sheffield, on the 21st July last. Mr Hardy and Mr Johnston were for the prosecution. Mr Dearsley and Mr Shepherd defended the prisoners. The circumstances were very similar to those stated in the previous case; in fact, it was in the course of this disturbance that the poor fellow whose death has just been inquired into, was killed. Several witnesses were called to prove the particular part which the prisoners severally took in the transaction. They were heard to urge the crowd on to violence, and themselves threw stones, and were heard to vow vengeance against the police. All the prisoners were found guilty.

Mr Baron Martin, in sentencing the prisoners, said that he had made his mind up to make an example of them, in order that the people of this country might see that the law should be upheld if possible. Here were six men belonging to a large body of people resident in this country – he alluded to the Irish – who, obliged to leave their own country because of its poverty, came over to this country, where they enjoyed better wages and other great advantages which they could not have at home, and yet they could not keep quiet, but must need display their gratitude by breaking the peace of this country and indulging in all sorts of riot and acts of violence. He considered Burke the worst of the party engaged in this transaction, he having thrown the stone which in all probability killed the policeman, and also having struck another man with a stone in a stocking and stabbed him in the arm with a knife. The sentence upon him, therefore, was that he be transported for fifteen years. As to Smith, he considered him quite as bad, he having beat a man whilst he was almost dead, and then sworn upon the remonstrance of his own daughter that he would murder him; but the law would not allow him to give the same punishment as Burke. He, however, should give him two years' imprisonment, with hard labour; and the four other prisoners, Dunlevy, McCormack, Charleston, and Finnerty, must be severally imprisoned for 12 months with hard labour.

The court proceedings seem rather strange. Burke and Dunlevy entered the court facing a capital charge of the wilful murder of a policeman, and yet after hearing all the evidence and being found guilty of manslaughter, the two prisoners received sentences of fifteen years' transportation and twelve months' penal servitude with hard labour respectively. Given the circumstances surrounding the death, a manslaughter verdict was probably the correct one, although the actions of Burke in striking another man with a stone in a stocking and stabbing him in the arm with a knife, suggests a degree of premeditation. This, coupled with his alleged vow that he would 'kill the ------ watchman', indicates that Burke was relatively fortunate to receive the sentence he did. And Dunlevy, who was also guilty of the offence of manslaughter, got just twelve months with hard labour. Note also that the three men found guilty of manslaughter in the 'Owlerton Feast' case a year earlier received sentences of six months' penal servitude following a prolonged, joint assault on a defenceless man, whereas Burke was sent to Australia for fifteen years. Rather a large disparity! Still, this was nineteenth-century Victorian 'justice' and prejudice and disdain were never far below the surface. After all, Burke was an Irish immigrant who had killed a policeman executing his duty; at Owlerton, Holroyd, Haines and Knowles had beaten to death merely a poor saw grinder.

CHAPTER 8

THE AVOIDABLE DEATH OF OLIVIA SPOONER, WALKLEY, 1858

'The girl sank under the influences of cold and want of nourishment'

This report appeared in the *Manchester Guardian* on April 1, 1858:

SHOCKING CASE OF DEATH FROM WANT.
(From our Correspondent).

On Monday evening Mr. Badger, coroner, held an inquest at Walkley, in the outskirts of Sheffield, on view of the body of Olivia Spooner, aged 15 years, daughter of Edward Spooner, table-knife hafter. The circumstances of the young girl's death are of a painful character. Her mother died several years ago, leaving a husband and six children,

The husband was stated to have been a most intemperate man, and though the deceased and one or two of the sons helped him in the shop, the family were ill prepared to bear the privations consequent on bad trade which followed the panic of last year. The children were described by the neighbours as appearing half 'clammed' during the time of good trade. By the joint exertions of the father and the elder children, the family managed to subsist without parish relief until two months ago, when the father, being out of work, applied for relief. As only two children were under nine years of age, he was allowed 5s a week (half of it in bread) for them and himself, with the option of sending the children into the workhouse, of which he did not avail himself. He continued in receipt of parochial relief for three weeks, and this, he said, was the only period during which they suffered actual want, seven persons having to subsist on the 5s and such odd pence as the children could earn. He afterwards obtained work for a fortnight, in the last week of which he and the elder children earned 15s. Of this sum he spent 10d on drink, and paid 5s for shop and house rent. On returning home he fell down the steps leading to his house and severely injured himself. After lying ill for a week he obtained an order and was attended by Mr Wilson, the surgeon for Ecclesall union, in which he resided. For the deceased, who had been poorly for some weeks previous to his accident, and extremely ill all the time subsequently, he obtained no aid beyond occasionally getting her a half-pennyworth of aniseed, a pennyworth of stomach pills, and on one or two occasions two-pennyworth of rum, and could provide her with no food she could take.

Though the union surgeon was in attendance upon himself, it was not until Tuesday (yesterday) week that he requested the surgeon to see her, or called in a neighbour to do anything for her. Mr Wilson found the poor creature lying upon an old filthy mattress, with nothing to cover her but a very few pieces of wearing apparel, disgustingly filthy. During the first week after the father's accident, two of the children had earned 10s, but little or nothing afterwards; and, in the subsequent week, a neighbour woman had obtained parish relief for the father alone, who had made no application to the parish, on behalf of his family. The parish officers were, in fact, totally ignorant that they were in want. When, however, Mr Wilson visited the deceased, and saw the destitute condition of the family, he at once wrote an urgent letter to Mr Dearden, the relieving officer, requesting him to remove the family at once to the workhouse. Mr Dearden, early next morning, sent an officer with a cab and blankets, to effect their removal, but the father replied that he was not going to the workhouse, 'for him or for any other parish bulldog', and when the officer became urgent, he put a poker in the fire to heat, and threatened to run it through him.

Mr Dearden, next day, sent another officer, to try to persuade the man to go into the workhouse, but it was then too late, for she was already in a dying state, and expired the same evening. On going to view the body, which was in a shockingly emaciated condition, the jury found the house in a most filthy and desolate state. It stands on the north side *of a high hill, quite exposed to the north-west winds, which, during the late severe weather, must have acted with terrible severity on the poor girl and the other ragged half-fed inmates. The father's only excuse for refusing to go to the workhouse was that he had received no previous notice of the intention to remove him, and that his children cried. It appeared that several of the children were ill during the severe weather, and that the father had repelled the approaches of his neighbours, by whom the sufferings of the family would otherwise have been earlier made known and relieved. It was the general opinion that shame at the state of his house had prevented the father from earlier calling in assistance.*

Mr Wilson was confident that the death of the girl had been accelerated by want of proper necessaries of both food and clothing; but, not having made a post-mortem examination of the body, he could not absolutely swear that it had been altogether caused by privation. The jury returned a verdict that death had been accelerated by want, blaming the father for not sooner procuring her medical aid.

Poor Olivia Spooner, who lived her pitiful life in the Bole Hill area of Sheffield, was buried at Wardsend Cemetery, Owlerton.

The 'panic' referred to in the reports, which produced 'bad trade', was the 1857 financial crisis brought about by the rapid over-expansion of the United States economy. By the mid-1850s the world's economy was becoming inter-dependent and thus the crisis spread to Britain, where Lord Palmerston's government was forced to forego the requirements of the 1844 Peel Banking Act, which required the maintenance of sufficient gold and silver reserves to match the amount of cash in circulation. The world economy did not recover for a number of years, only fully doing so after the American Civil War of 1861-65.

The Ecclesall union, at which Mr Wilson was surgeon, was at Nether Edge, on the site that later became Nether Edge Hospital.

CHAPTER 9

THE STRANGE DEATH OF ARTHUR ALLEN, FARGATE, 1866

'I have hammered him with the hammer, and stabbed him with a knife'

Arthur Allen was buried at Sheffield's General Cemetery on November 24, 1866. He was just eighteen years old. He died on November 22, two days after he was attacked by a boy called Henry Gabbitas. The *Leeds Mercury* of November 21 relates the events leading to Arthur's death:

> ## DREADFUL MURDER BY A BOY AT SHEFFIELD.
>
> A horrible and most singular crime was committed at Sheffield yesterday morning by a boy sixteen years of age, his victim being a fellow apprentice and bedfellow, about eighteen years old.

Mr Draper, a very respectable draper, of Barker Pool, has several apprentices, who live at his house adjoining the shop. Of these, Henry Gabbitas was the junior, and Arthur Allen was the next above him. They slept together in one of the garrets of the house, another apprentice, named Stephen Moss, sleeping in the next room. On Monday night Gabbitas was unusually silent at supper, and complained of being unwell. But the family were undisturbed during the night, and had no idea of the tragedy that awaited them in the morning. About half past seven, Gabbitas went to the bedroom door of Mr Draper and said, 'I have killed Arthur.' 'What?' 'I have killed Arthur. I have done it for revenge.' 'What can you mean?' said Mr Draper. Gabbitas replied, 'I have hammered him with the hammer, and stabbed him with a knife.' Mr Draper hurried upstairs and found Allen lying on his back on the bed, and weltering in blood. He was totally insensible. Mr Farrell, of Norfolk Street, and Dr Younge, of Norfolk Row, were sent for, and very quickly attended, but only to find that the case was hopeless. Allen's head is severely fractured, and he has lain since quite unconscious. The only sound he has uttered has been occasionally faintly to say 'Oh!' and once or twice he has opened an eye.

Gabbitas said that he committed the dreadful deed about 5.30, when the watchmen were about going off their beats, and that he afterwards went to the police office to give himself up but, thinking that he should not be believed, he did not go in, but returned to Fargate, and told Mr Draper. He walked again to the police office with a senior apprentice, Stephen Moss, talking freely and with apparent composure by the way. At the police office he began to say that he gave himself up for killing Allen, but could not finish, and Moss completed the statement. Gabbitas was left in custody, and a policeman returned with Moss to Fargate. He found in the bedroom the hammer and the knife. The hammer was one Mr Draper had used about five on Monday afternoon in opening a box. Two hours after, when it was wanted again, it could not be found. It now appears that Gabbitas had secreted it for his murderous purpose. The knife was a nine-inch carving knife, which had been used at supper on Monday night.

The origin of this sad affair is a matter of conjecture. Gabbitas had the character of a good boy, and there did not appear to be anything morose or dangerous in his disposition. He and Allen were very good friends, and on Monday night appeared to be particularly so. Mr Draper's conjecture is that the anger of Gabbitas had been aroused by the fact that he had been engaged with Allen in some irregularities, which had led to an order that they should not go out at night. Gabbitas is supposed to have blamed Allen for this, but the supposition does not harmonise with the appearance of friendship that Gabbitas showed on Monday night. He must, however, have been capable of great duplicity, for he had then no doubt secreted the hammer with which he first attacked the victim.

The wounds are on the left side of the head and neck, and there is, therefore, no doubt that the first blow was given while Allen was sleeping, and given so effectually that he uttered no cry. Gabbitas has been remanded by the magistrates awaiting the certain death of his victim. Gabbitas is the son of a painter at Hull.

The *Manchester Guardian* then reported that Arthur Allen had now died, and informed its readers of details of the inquest:

THE SHEFFIELD TRAGEDY

The youth Allen, who was so savagely attacked as he lay in bed by a fellow apprentice, named Gabbitas, died at Sheffield, yesterday morning. On Wednesday, about the middle of the day, he appeared to rally a little. He was very slightly conscious, and the pulse rose somewhat. He spoke several times, mentioning the name of Gabbitas. During the afternoon, however, he again became totally unconscious, and remained in this condition up to the time of his death.

The inquest was held yesterday. The prisoner was brought in by several police officers, and was placed at a table in the centre of the room, next to a table reserved for witnesses. The attention of all present was immediately concentrated upon him, but he maintained a surprising firmness and composure for some time. He is very youthful in appearance, and it would defy the most acute physiognomist to detect any trace of malignant passion in his thoughtful and mild countenance. After the examination of the witnesses had proceeded for a short space, the prisoner's firmness gave way, and frequent bursts of weeping showed that he realised the position in which he was placed. His distress was greatest when the officer produced the hammer and the knife with which the murder had been committed. He shrank away with shuddering repugnance; his breathing became quick and laboured, and he seemed to be overpowered with horror. He has stated that he 'always felt that he should murder somebody, but he did not know who it was to be'. He was a fatalist; and having accepted as something inevitable the belief that he should come to the ignominious death of a murderer, he made no attempt to resist the temptation that constantly beset him to bring about the realisation of his awful belief.

His account of the manner in which the murder was committed is shocking beyond expression. He had contemplated it for a week, and on the fatal night the weapons he used were secreted beneath the very pillow on which he allowed his victim to repose in unsuspecting confidence. He sat up during the whole night in the bed, watching the poor lad. His stepmother's prediction seemed to ring in his ears, and after that awful vigil he resolved, just as the day dawned, to commit the deed. It is consistent with all that he has previously said, to learn now from his own lips, that he 'repeated the Lord's Prayer, and then struck the blow'. That blow took effect on the left side of the neck, just beneath the ear, and the injury caused by the hammer was increased by a severe stab with the carving knife. The blow was so violent that the blade snapped in half. Two other wounds were inflicted with the hammer, each of them fracturing the skull; but the first was the immediate cause of death.

Mr Farrell, the surgeon who was called in to attend the deceased, gave the following evidence: 'The deceased was in a totally unconscious state from wounds. There was a wound about two inches in extent on the left temple, another upon the crown of the head, and another under the left ear. There were no wounds on the breast or the body; there was one on the side of the neck, which I have mentioned as being below the ear. The first wound showed a fracture and depression of the skull, the temporal bone was broken off and driven in upon the brain by the violence of the blow. The second wound was a fracture of the crown of the head, a simple fracture from a blow, which had not displaced or crushed the bone. The third was a superficial wound of the neck. Some of the large vessels within were ruptured, and bleeding was going on to a great extent inwardly. The first wound was the cause of death, no doubt. The fractures were produced by a blunt instrument, and the wound on the neck by a knife.'

The jury returned a verdict of wilful murder. The prisoner was then removed. He seemed to have regained his composure, and moved quietly through the throng of persons to the cab in which he was removed.

The case was sent to Leeds Assizes and was heard on December 18, 1866, four weeks after the fatality. A report of the trial appeared the following day in *The Scotsman*:

THE SHEFFIELD MURDER
A YOUTH SENTENCED TO DEATH AT LEEDS
Before Justice Lush, at Leeds, Henry Gabbitas, aged sixteen, was indicted for murdering Arthur Allen at Sheffield. The prisoner and deceased were fellow apprentices with a Sheffield draper, and, last November, there was some little disagreement or ill-feeling between them, in consequence of Allen having informed their employer where

they spent their evenings after business hours. Prisoner conceived some resentful feeling against him in consequence, and on the night in question took a hammer and knife to bed with him; and whilst Allen was asleep struck him twice on the head with the hammer, and then stabbed him.

The defence set up was 'homicidal mania', and a low type of physical and mental development; the latter intensified by epileptic attacks to which he had been subject, and also to a general depression of spirits from ill-treatment on the part of a stepmother from an early period of his life. Two 'mad doctors' were called in to express an opinion in support of this theory. Their evidence was of the usual nature, and was characterised by the Judge as 'metaphysical and ultra-refined' with respect to subtle distinctions and gradations of insanity.

After Mr Campbell Foster had elaborately replied to the defence, the jury found the prisoner guilty, but recommended him to mercy on account of his youth. The ladies in the gallery sobbed whilst his Lordship, who was also affected, passed sentence. He said he would not trust himself to comment upon the awfulness of having to pass sentence on a criminal so young. He would forward the recommendation to mercy to the proper quarter; but his duty was simply to pronounce the sentence of the law, which his Lordship did in voice broken by emotion.

The convict received the judgement without moving a muscle, and descended the steps from the court into the cell below as lightly and as freely as if he were passing into the outer world, instead of into the gloomy and fearful recess of the condemned cell.

It must have been very rare for a judge to break down when sentencing a person to death. Henry Gabbitas, on the other hand, seemingly was not affected one bit and disassociated himself from the proceedings. However, execution records show that the death sentence was not carried out, so it must be assumed that the Home Secretary accepted the jury's recommendation for mercy. The length of time Gabbitas served in prison is not known, and Arthur Allen's grave sadly is no longer visible. Finally, it is a shame that *The Scotsman* report does not give any details as to the identities or qualifications of the two 'mad doctors' called to give evidence in Gabbitas's defence!

CHAPTER 10

THE ACCIDENTAL DEATH OF AN EMINENT ENGINEER, ABBEYDALE ROAD, 1869

'Oh, my father is killed!'

On May 5, 1869, the *Sheffield and Rotherham Independent* printed the following report:

SERIOUS CARRIAGE ACCIDENT ON THE ABBEY-DALE ROAD.—A very serious accident happened on Wednesday afternoon to John Shortridge, Esq., of Chipping House, Abbeydale road. Mr. Shortridge was driving home from Baslow with his daughter, Mrs. Sellars, and when near the works of Mr. Tyzack the horse took fright—at what is not known—and commenced to kick and plunge in a very alarming manner.

After smashing the splashboard and otherwise damaging the carriage, and tearing off the shoes of its hind feet, the animal made a sudden plunge and overturned the vehicle, throwing its occupants out upon the road. Unfortunately, the carriage fell upon Mr Shortridge, and was dragged off him by the horse, which started at a great pace. Mr Shortridge and Mrs Sellars were removed as speedily as possible, and were attended by Dr Thompson and Mr Waterhouse. Mr Shortridge

59

was found to have sustained very serious injuries. Three of his ribs and his collar-bone were broken, and from a large scalp wound blood flowed profusely. All that medical skill could suggest was done, and the unfortunate gentleman yesterday morning appeared rather better. Towards noon, however, a change for the worse set in, and last night, we regret to say, he was lying in a very precarious state. Mrs Sellars was severely bruised and shaken; but, happily, her injuries were of a much less serious character. The horse, which had only been in Mr Shortridge's possession a short time, escaped unhurt, but the carriage was smashed to pieces.

Shortridge died three days after the accident. The Coroner, Mr Webster, opened an inquest at Shortridge's spacious home, where it was learned that the frightened horse had been out only once prior to this journey. Furthermore, Mr Shortridge's groom had advised his employer not to use the animal. William Oates, a cab driver travelling behind the Shortridge carriage, told the inquest that he had seen the horse uncontrollably increasing its speed, so much so that he lost sight of it as it rounded a bend. He arrived on the scene to find Mrs Sellars in the road, her face bleeding. Mr Shortridge was lying nearby, the horse and carriage nowhere to be seen. Mrs Sellars exclaimed, 'Oh, my father is killed!' Oates and his two passengers carried the injured man and his daughter to their home.

Mr Waterhouse attended Shortridge until his death, at 7pm on May 8. The cause of death, he said, 'had probably occurred from some internal rupture caused by the accident and Mr Shortridge had died suddenly in convulsions after being raised to get an easier position.' The jury returned a verdict of accidental death. John Shortridge was buried at Heeley Parish Church on May 11, 1869. The funeral was reported the next day by the *Sheffield and Rotherham Independent*:

FUNERAL OF MR JOHN SHORTRIDGE
The remains of the late Mr John Shortridge, of Chipping House, Abbeydale, who came to his death from injuries received by his horse taking fright and overturning the carriage while driving home from Baslow, were interred yesterday, at noon, in the family vault, in Heeley churchyard. The hearse was followed by four mourning coaches, and seven private carriages. The funeral service was read by the Rev. H. D. Jones, who delivered a short but impressive address. The pall bearers were Mr L. Miller, Mr H. Wright, Mr J. Chambers, and Mr Cocking. There were also present Aldermen Jessop, Carr, Jackson, and other members of the Town Council. The coffin was supplied by Mr

Hawkesley, Bridgehouses, and the whole of the arrangements, which were under the personal superintendence of Mr Grundy, High Street, gave great satisfaction. The stone which covers the entrance to the vault is of immense size and ponderous weight, viz. twenty one tons. We have pleasure in stating that Mrs Sellars, who was with her father at the time of the accident, has nearly recovered from the injuries she received. Very great sympathy is expressed for Mrs Shortridge in her sad bereavement.

The funeral must have been some sight, with twelve horse-drawn carriages in procession and several local dignitaries in attendance. The stone 'of immense size and ponderous weight' is a tall granite obelisk, which required twenty horses to haul into position. The inscription at its base reads:

JOHN SHORTRIDGE
BORN 16TH MARCH 1803. DIED 7TH MAY 1869.
IN LOVING MEMORY OF FAITH
BELOVED WIFE OF THE LATE WILLIAM SHORTRIDGE
DIED DEC 28TH 1929 AGED 88 YEARS

There was once another inscription higher up the memorial, but this portion is made from sandstone and has weathered badly, so it cannot be deciphered.

John Shortridge was 66 years old at the time of his death. He was a renowned engineer and industrialist, co-owning with William Howell the Hartford Steel Works, built on the Wicker in 1853. The works were severely damaged by the 1864 Sheffield Flood, after which Shortridge claimed £1,016 8s 6d in compensation from the Sheffield Waterworks Company. He settled for £1,000. Two years later the business was bought by an even more famous Sheffield steelmaker, Samuel Osborne. The offices fronting on to the Wicker are now the premises of the Sheffield and District Afro-Caribbean Community Association (SADACCA). A street at Attercliffe was named after Shortridge (it runs between Attercliffe Road and Chippingham Street). He was variously described as a railway contractor and a brickmaker, and was influential in the building of Wicker Arches, the Sheffield to Manchester railway and was responsible for the introduction of the first horse-drawn tram route from the town centre to the Red Lion public house at Heeley.

Shortridge was the eldest son of his family and inherited some property from his maternal grandfather in Cumberland in the 1830s. He was born in this part of the country, at Kingcreahill, Bewcastle, and married Ellen Leach, of Chipping, north Lancashire, on June 14, 1826. Ellen was almost four years older than John, being born on November 17, 1799. John first developed business interests in Liverpool and Glossop before moving to Sheffield some time before 1849. He first made a home in the town on Cricket Inn Road. His work on the new railway system must have earned him good money, for he then paid £3,300 for land described as being 'the Lathe Field, the Plantation, the North and South Crofts and the toll house', just off Abbeydale Road. Here he built a two-storey mansion and named it 'Chipping House', after the home village of his wife. The house, which had large gardens and entrance gates opening on to Abbeydale Road, was demolished for the building of new housing around 1891. 'The works of Mr Tyzack', described in the newspaper report of the accident as being where his horse first took fright, is now Abbeydale Industrial Hamlet.

Ellen Shortridge died just two months after the death of her husband, in Retford, Nottinghamshire, where she may have gone to mourn, perhaps staying with relatives. She was also buried at Heeley Parish Church. One can imagine that she died of a broken heart.

The grave of John Shortridge at Heeley Parish Church

CHAPTER 11

THE VIOLENT DEATH OF SERGEANT GIBSON, SHEFFIELD TOWN CENTRE, 1872

'His helmet was placed on his doorstep cut to pieces, and had chalked on it the word "death"'

William Beardshaw was the first Sheffield policeman to die while exercising his duty, in 1855 (see Chapter 7). Seventeen years later Police Sergeant Samuel Pidd Gibson, aged 33, became the second. The *Leeds Mercury* of April 6, 1872 gave details of the incident that led to his death in a report of the subsequent court case:

CHARGE OF MURDER AT SHEFFIELD
Samuel Walker (27), table blade grinder, was indicted for the wilful murder Sergeant Pidd Gibson, at Sheffield. Mr Waddy, Mr Barker and Mr Wilberforce appeared for the prosecution; Mr Blackburn and Mr Nyalls were retained for the defence. Prisoner pleaded 'Not guilty'.

Mr Waddy, in opening the case for the prosecution, said the murdered man was a policeman at Sheffield. On the night of the 25th of December Gibson, in company with another policeman named Pearson, was in Coulston Street, at the bottom of Snig Hill, in Sheffield, when they were informed that a disturbance was taking place in Spring Street, in the vicinity, it being made by a man named Kennywell. In order to secure Kennywell between them, the officers entered Spring

Street, at different ends, and near to the Bird-in-Hand public house they met again. Kennywell was secured, handcuffed, and was taken away towards the Town Hall. When they had got a short distance an attempt was made by the crowd to rescue the prisoner, and in the course of the attempt Gibson was struck a violent blow on the left side of the head, and the person who struck the blow, according to the evidence of witnesses which he (Mr Waddy) would call, was the prisoner. It was not anticipated at first that that the wound inflicted on Gibson would prove fatal, but an abscess formed, and it was found necessary to perform a surgical operation, by which a piece of the skull was cut clean out, but it was too late, and a short time afterwards Gibson died. Gibson in the struggle lost his helmet, and some time afterwards it was placed on his doorstep cut to pieces, and had chalked on it the word 'death'.

At the close of the evidence for the prosecution, Mr Blackburn, in an able speech, addressed the jury for the defence. Referring to the time which elapsed between the assault upon Gibson and proceedings being taken against the prisoner, he said it was inconceivable that nothing should have been done for two months to bring the prisoner to justice if Gibson and Pearson were certain that prisoner dealt the blow. He suggested a theory accounting for the blow dealt at the deceased man, which was perfectly consistent with prisoner's innocence; and urged upon the jury that the evidence called for the prosecution was unworthy of credit.

His Lordship, in summing up the evidence, said that the fact of such a length of time having been allowed to elapse between the night Gibson received his injuries and the apprehension – after Gibson's death – of the prisoner was not to be accounted for by the argument used for the prosecution, that they did not consider Gibson was in danger. It was alleged that, on the very night of the assault, the police knew that it had been done by 'Grinder Joe', and yet no steps were taken either to have him up for unlawful wounding or for common assault. The question, therefore, had been very fairly put by the counsel for the prisoner, what did that indicate to the mind of any reasonable man? Could it be explained on any other hypothesis than that those two men (Pearson and Gibson) were doubtful as to whether prisoner was the man or not? Then there was the other extraordinary circumstance, that Kennywell was charged with assault, the two policemen gave evidence against him, he was convicted, and yet not a single word was said about the prisoner. Taking those matters into consideration, and also remembering that, apart from the lighted lamps, the night was dark, there was a large crowd pressing upon the police, there was scuffling and great confusion, it was a question as to whether they could believe the witnesses Sweeny and Harriet – who positively swore the prisoner was the man who dealt the blow – or not. His Lordship concluded by pointing out to the jury the great responsibility that devolved upon them, the necessity of carefully weighing the evidence, and their duty of returning a verdict of guilty if they were convinced on the evidence of prisoner's guilt, and of finding a verdict of not guilty if they disbelieved the evidence, or even if they had any reasonable doubt.

The jury, without retiring, acquitted the prisoner.

Spring Street, where the disturbance involving Kennywell took place, runs from the bottom of Snig Hill, across Corporation Street and joins Bower Street, near to West Bar. One of the police officers must have run around to enter Spring Street from Bower Street, while the other entered from Snig Hill. At the time of this incident the area was thick with housing, small workshops and public houses, but today is just wasteland, car parks and the occasional building. The Town Hall towards which Kennywell was taken was not the current building (which was completed in 1897), but the old Town Hall at the bottom of Waingate, which later became the law courts and is now in a state of disrepair. And it will not have gone unnoticed that the incident that led to Sergeant Gibson's death occurred on Christmas night. In all probability, for some poorer sections of Victorian society, the festive period mattered little and was indistinguishable from any other time of year.

CHAPTER 12

THE UNTIMELY DEATHS OF GEORGE GEE AND WILLIAM MASSEY, BRIDGEHOUSES, 1873

'He does not seem to have known that the train was so near'

The gravestone of George Gee in the churchyard of Christ Church, Stannington, is still in remarkably good condition for its age. Even more unusual is the verse that accompanies details of George's death:

> *DEATH DID TO ME SHORT WARNING GIVE*
> *THEREFORE BE CAREFUL HOW YOU LIVE*
> *PREPARE IN TIME, DO NOT DELAY*
> *FOR I WAS QUICKLY CALLED AWAY*
> *IN AFFECTIONATE REMEMBRANCE OF*
> *GEORGE GEE*
> *WHO WAS A GUARD ON THE M.S. & L. RAILWAY AND WAS*
> *ACCIDENTALLY KILLED AT THE VICTORIA, SHEFFIELD ON 27TH*
> *DECEMBER 1873*
> *AGED 24 YEARS*

The *Birmingham Daily Post* of December 29, 1873 reported bare details of what happened:

On Saturday afternoon a goods guard, named George Gee, was killed near the Victoria Railway Station, at Sheffield. He was walking along the line, when he was knocked down by some trucks. The same day a young man, named William Massey, in the employ of the company, was knocked down by an express train on its way to Manchester. He sustained frightful injuries, which must prove fatal.

The *Sheffield and Rotherham Independent* of January 3, 1874 added further information about the accidents. By this time William Massey had indeed died.

FATAL ACCIDENTS AT BRIDGEHOUSES
Gee was removed to the Infirmary, where he died soon after his admission. His injuries consisted of a compound comminuted fracture of the right thigh, dislocation of the left thigh, and a compound comminuted fracture of the left arm. The same afternoon a number taker, William Massey, 16 years of age, was knocked down by the 1.56 express train to Manchester. He was engaged in taking the numbers of some carriages a short distance from the station, and does not seem to have known that the train was so near. He sustained a compound comminuted fracture of the leg, a scalp wound, and a compound fracture of the arm. He died at the Infirmary on Monday. An inquest on both the deceased was opened by Mr D. Wightman, on Tuesday.

All rather gruesome! It is doubtful whether such detailed explanations of injuries suffered by an accident victim would be given today.

CHAPTER 13

DEATH BY CORPORAL PUNISHMENT, PARK, 1878

'Seven months ago she was struck on the face and the back of the head by a teacher'

The following disturbing report appeared in the *Manchester Guardian* on September 25, 1878:

ALLEGED VIOLENCE IN A SCHOOL BOARD SCHOOL.

The Sheffield Coroner opened an inquest yesterday on the body of Isabella Buckley, ten years of age. The deceased was a scholar at the Park Board School, Norwich-street, and it was alleged that about seven months ago she was struck on the face and back of the head by a teacher, Miss Asman, and that ever since then she had been ill and subject to convulsive fits.

She was, it was further stated, again struck by another teacher at the same school four months ago, and since then had gradually sunk. The School Board was represented by its Clerk, Mr J. F. Moss, and Mr Davis, its inspector of schools. Deceased's mother stated that her daughter had told her that Miss Asman had hit her over the cheek and on the back of the neck. Two children corroborated the evidence as to part of the alleged violence. Miss Asman, who has since got married and left the school, denied the charge. The case was adjourned. The Coroner said he did not adjourn the inquiry in the hope of getting any additional evidence, but that the public might not be able to say that the inquest had in any way been hurried over. It would also give Mrs Steer (Miss Asman) the opportunity to bring any evidence she thought proper, although he might tell her that the evidence of the surgeon who had made the post-mortem examination cleared her entirely from any criminality. He said the disease might have come on naturally and the jury could not possibly, after such a statement as that, find anything against Mrs Steer.

The *Daily News* of the same day gave some details not included in the *Guardian's* report:

ALLEGED DEATH FROM PUNISHMENT IN A BOARD SCHOOL
The evidence was to the effect that seven months since the deceased asked a pupil teacher, Miss Asman, to be allowed to go into the yard. Permission was refused, and a short time afterwards she again asked, inasmuch as she required to leave the room. Miss Asman still refused, and struck her on the face and back and at the head. When school was over the deceased went home, and was soon afterwards found by her father in the closet in a fit. From this she did not recover for several hours, and ever since then she had been unwell, subject to fits, and complained of severe pains in her head. She died on Saturday. The surgeon who had attended her during her illness certifies that death was primarily the result of violence, and the medical gentleman who made a post-mortem examination said death was caused by serious effusion to the brain, the result of violence, or from natural violence. The teacher admitted she was unaware of a rule forbidding corporal punishment until the offence and the punishment had been first recorded.

The *Liverpool Mercury* briefly reported the jury's verdict in its edition of September 28, 1878:

The inquest on the body of Isabella Buckley, aged ten, whose death is alleged to have been caused by corporal punishment, inflicted in a board school at Sheffield, was concluded on Thursday. An Open Verdict was returned, the jury expressing a strong opinion that the school board should prevent corporal punishment.

An 'open verdict' is a finding by a coroner's jury of death without stating the cause. It strictly means that the jury confirms that the death is suspicious but is unable to reach any of the other verdicts open to it. It therefore affirms that a crime has been committed without stating by whom.

Based purely on these newspaper reports it seems that Florence Asman was extremely fortunate not to face criminal charges. It must be admitted that the case against her was based on allegations from Isabella's mother, Sarah, who did not see the actual attack, and two of Isabella's school friends, who stated that they did witness the assault. The cause of death was 'serious effusion to the brain', but whether this was due to natural causes or the alleged assault the jury could not decide, and therefore returned an open verdict. Perhaps Florence should have been at least arrested and charged for the alleged offence. It is clear that the jury were uneasy about the verdict, as they issued a strong recommendation to the School Board requesting that they should exercise great vigilance in ensuring that the rules were kept. In other words, it was implied that Miss Asman did assault Isabella, otherwise why was such advice issued?

Two other fairly minor points are worth noting. There is no indication that Isabella was a sick child prior to the assault. The 1881 Census seems to indicate that her family was exceedingly robust, especially given the rampant child mortality rates in the district. Second, the assault seems to have occurred just around the time Florence Asman was getting married to William Steer. Knowing that she was leaving the school, as was the norm when getting married, was she unduly stressed at the time, and lost her temper with Isabella? Pure conjecture of course, but if the case had gone to court, the lingering suspicion that an assault had occurred would have been resolved one way or the other.

The 1871 Census showed Florence Asman living with her parents, Wilfred and Marina, at No.81 Washington Road, in the Sharrow District. After her marriage to William Steer the couple resided at No.34 Kearsley Road, Highfield. There was a son, Albert, aged seven, and a live-in servant, Annie Jackson, aged nineteen. Albert was therefore either born out of wedlock or was not Florence's son. By 1891 they had moved to No.651 Queen's Road, but Albert was not living with them, nor was there any domestic help. Ten years later they had moved again, to No.237 Abbeydale Road. William was now a clerk in the works of a silver plate manufacturer. It was to be his last appearance in the Census, for in 1911 Florence was a 51-year-old widow. Living with her was a twelve-year-old adopted daughter, Kate Elizabeth Steer. Florence lived to be the grand old age of 79. She died in March 1939, over sixty years after the death of Isabella Buckley.

Norwich Street in 2011. The school stood where the trees are to the left.

No.34 Kearsley Road, Highfield, the marital home of Florence Steer

The 1881 Census (three years after Isabella's death) shows the Buckley family living at No.77 Hague Lane. The family now consisted of father Robert (37), mother Sarah (35), and children Charles (15), Annie (10), Edward (7), Henry (5), Albert (3) and Walter (1). Isabella was therefore their second child.

The area around Hague Lane and Norwich Street, once dense with housing, was demolished for the building of Park Hill flats. Both roads are commemorated by 'streets in the sky', namely Hague Row and Norwich Row. Norwich Street crossed Hague Lane, then turned a dog-leg down the steep slope to Granville Street, which is now where the trams run behind the Midland Station. The school backed on to Granville Street, therefore it must have been situated on quite an incline. Some of Norwich Street remains, with its original cobblestones, but the area where the school once stood is now covered in vegetation.

CHAPTER 14

THE LONELY DEMISE OF THOMAS DICKINSON, GRENO WOODS, 1880

'A starved to death cripple, with finger bones bare'

In his book *Smithy Rhymes and Stithy Chimes: Or the Short and Simple Annals of the Poor, Spelt by the Unlettered Muse of Your Humble Bard*, Joseph Senior wrote this poem:

THERE'S SOME ONE TO BLAME:
A DIRGE FOR THE POOR CRIPPLE WHO WAS FOUND STARVED
TO DEATH IN GRENO WOOD, NEAR CHAPELTOWN, OCT. 24, 1880
A starved to death cripple, with finger bones bare,
Ah! perhaps his last supper was eaten from there;
Oh! my soul, what a shame!
By hunger's tooth gnaw'd to the supper of death,
Where o'er the lean viands this grace froze his breath,
There is some one to blame!
Who gave Hoary Sorrow hard cinders to break?
If earth won't for shattered humanity speak,
Oh ye Heav'ns, weep a flood!
Who spurned him when dying from shelter and bed,
To seek a cold pillow where brambles were spread,
In yon dark northern wood?

Had he been a prince or a lord of the soil,

Instead of a cripple who could not win oil
To keep life's lamp aflame,
The foulness would not have been cleared in a day,
O Britons, awake dozing justice, and say
There is some one to blame!
Hark, hark! that sad groan, as it wings from his tongue,
To the disc of God's throne, the angels are stung,
And cry 'shame, England, shame!'
Ye poor-law dispensers and jurymen too,
Who can't pity cripples, may God pity you,
And that some one is to blame.

The death of the poor, starving cripple is in fact a true story, as reported in the *Sheffield and Rotherham Independent* on October 25, 1880:

SHOCKING DISCOVERY IN GRENO WOOD
As Martin Dickinson, of Mortomley, near Chapeltown, was walking through Greno Wood, yesterday morning, he saw a man near the footpath, and on going to him found that he was dead. He communicated with Police Constable Ellerby, of Highgreen, who had him at once conveyed to the Crown Inn, to await a coroner's enquiry. It appeared that the deceased slept at Wortley Union, Grenoside, on Wednesday evening, and left that institution on Thursday morning. When admitted he gave the name of Thomas Dickinson, tailor, 67 years of age, a native of Staffordshire, and said he had walked from Sheffield, and intended going to Penistone on the Thursday morning. He walked with a crutch and a stick. On Thursday morning, when he left the Union, he proceeded with great difficulty as far as the Crown Inn, on the Wortley road, where he called and asked for refreshments, which were given him. He remained in the neighbourhood the greater part of the day, and the supposition is that he went into the wood to sleep, that he drew his coat over his head, and the night being exceedingly cold, was starved to death. When found his head was covered with his coat, his back was bare, and his finger ends were eaten on.

The assumption today would be that Thomas died due to lack of food. The fact that his finger ends were 'eaten on' also suggests that he was so hungry he was forced to eat bits of himself. However, that can't be the case as he had taken refreshments that morning at the Crown Inn. Older readers, especially those from Sheffield, may be aware of the alternative use of the word 'starved'. In this city the word was also used to mean 'cold', but that usage has gone out of fashion. In other words, Thomas Dickinson froze to death. But that doesn't explain his 'eaten on' fingers. Nibbled at by scavenging animals, perhaps, or was it frostbite?

Wortley Union Workhouse stood on Salt Box Lane, which runs between what is now Halifax Road and Main Street, Grenoside. A mental health facility, Grenoside Grange, now occupies the site. The Crown Inn, where Thomas consumed his last meal, still exists, near the junction of the A629 and the A61 at High Green.

One other point of note; Thomas's body was discovered by a man with the same surname, but there is no indication they were related – just coincidental.

CHAPTER 15

A ROMANTIC SUICIDE PACT, LOXLEY, 1881

'He was the first, and for five years he has been the last'

The Census record of the Shaw family, taken on the night of April 3, 1881, shows that they lived in a house on Hagg Lane. The head of the family was 27-year-old stone mason James. His wife was Mary, aged 24. They had three children: Frederick, aged four, Herbert, aged two, and John, aged one. Hagg Lane still exists but the house has long gone. As far can be ascertained, the other party in this tragic affair, Mary Wagstaffe, was not living at home in April 1881 but working as a domestic servant at the house of William Bentley at No.45 Owlerton Road.

Little over a month later both families would be ripped apart by the actions of the couple. In May, a local newspaper reported that a 'Romantic Double Suicide' had occurred in Rowell Wheel Dam in the Rivelin Valley, near Sheffield:

ROMANTIC DOUBLE SUICIDE.

On Thursday morning the bodies of James Shaw, mason and builder ; and a young woman, named Wagstaffe, were found in a dam in the Rivelin Valley, near Sheffield.

The two had known each other from their childhood, and some years ago Shaw wished to pay his addresses to the girl, but her parents raised a strong objection to the courtship, and it was broken off, and Shaw married another woman. It is believed that an illicit friendship had been kept up between Shaw and the girl Wagstaffe. On Monday they eloped, and came to Sheffield, where they remained till Wednesday night, when they returned to the neighbourhood of their homes, and, early on Thursday morning, tied their hands together with a piece of braid and threw themselves into the dam. The girl had written two letters in pencil – one to her parents and the other to Shaw's wife – in one saying she would soon be no more, and in the other telling Mrs Shaw that she (Wagstaffe) was the only woman Shaw had ever loved. Shaw was 27 years of age, and his paramour three years younger.

The report was followed by another concerning the inquest into the couple's deaths:

THE TRAGEDY NEAR SHEFFIELD
The Sheffield coroner on Friday held an inquest at the Admiral Rodney Inn, Loxley, near Sheffield, on the bodies of James Shaw and Mary Wagstaffe, whose bodies were found in Rowell Wheel Dam on Thursday morning. Shaw, who was a married man, maintained an intimacy with the girl Wagstaffe. In early life they were sweethearts, and would have been married had the girl's mother not interfered. Shaw and the girl disappeared on Monday and were supposed to have eloped to America but after spending two nights in Sheffield they returned to Loxley valley on Thursday morning, and deliberately drowned themselves in a dam. Shaw could neither read nor write, but the girl could do both, and before committing suicide she wrote two letters in the dark by the water side, which were picked up by a boy and read at the inquest. The first ran thus:

'Dear father and mother, I hope you will forgive us, as you know he was the first, and for five years he has been the last. When we heard that someone had been asking about us at the Pack Horse [the public house where they stopped at Sheffield] it made us determined that if we could not live together, we should die together. I hope you won't fret about me, as I think we shall be better contented. This has been written in the dark. It was no use trying to keep us apart. I am sure that I will die without a pang, so now we do the end ourselves with love to all.'

The second letter was addressed to Mrs James Shaw, Rivelin, near Sheffield, and though written by the girl, professed to come from her husband. It stated:

'Dear wife, I now write a few lines to tell you the end and the cause for doing so. My companion was the first girl and the only girl that I have ever really loved, and I could not settle without her. Therefore it has caused me to do what I have done. I respect my children; hope someone will be kind to them, as I would like them to be brought up right. Hope no one will cast any reflections on their father's account. Give my love to my father and mother, and fare you well.'

It was disclosed in evidence that Shaw, who was a master mason and contractor, had been in pecuniary difficulties, and had threatened to commit suicide. About an hour before the couple flung themselves into the dam, a policeman had heard a male voice repeat several times, 'Come along, come along!' as if encouraging somebody in the way. Before taking the fatal plunge, the girl had loosened the braid from her hair and fastened her wrist to Shaw's arm and thus they died. The jury returned a verdict that the deceased had committed suicide by drowning, but as to the state of mind at the time there was not sufficient evidence.

A report in the *Illustrated Police News* stated that Mrs Shaw had no knowledge of her husband's indiscretions. He had recently been drinking heavily and left the house on Monday morning appearing dejected, though he made sure to kiss the children before departing. He said to his wife that he had a good mind to drown himself. This report also contained details of the couple's funerals:

INTERMENT OF THE SUICIDES
Relatives of Shaw and Wagstaffe are interred in the churchyard at Stannington, and it was decided that their bodies should be placed near the remains of departed kin. It was but natural to expect that crowds of people would gather near the church and witness the mournful proceedings of placing the bodies of persons who had gained such notoriety by their conduct and fatal act, into the earth. It had been arranged that the service of burial should commence at five o'clock, and for fully three hours before that time the churchyard was thronged with people, and the scene was somewhat of 'a fair'. In the lane near the church young men and maidens wandered about, some discussing the tragedy, others finding the intended execution of Hall a theme for conversation.

The two inns of the village were crowded by 'bona fide travellers', and the respective landlords were as busy serving refreshments as it was possible for them to be. The body of Shaw was the first to arrive, it being placed in the church at half-past four. It was conveyed in a Shillibeer from the house of Mr Shaw, senior, Dyke's Hall Road. The vehicle also contained the widow of the deceased man, his father and mother, several of his sisters, and two of his children. Upon its arrival at the church gate the coffin was carried, not without considerable difficulty, so great was the crowd, into the church, and placed in the centre aisle. Shaw's relatives occupied seats in five pews on the right of the nave, and there awaited the arrival of the coffin containing the remains of Wagstaffe, which did not take place until ten minutes after five o'clock. It was brought from the residence of her mother at Stoors, in the Bradfield hearse, her relatives being conveyed in a wagonette and two traps.

The coffin was met at the gate by the Vicar, who proceeded to read part of the Burial Service. That portion of the service appointed to be read inside the church being over, a rush was made by the occupants of the galleries down the tower steps into the graveyard, whither the corpse of Wagstaffe had been carried. The males clapped their hats on their heads and ran to the head of the steps, when the noise attendant upon such a crush was again heard. The coffin was carried to the north-east end of the churchyard, and interred in ground adjacent to the family grave. A wreath of flowers had been placed upon the plate, which bore the simple inscription: 'Mary Ann Wagstaffe, died May 19, 1881, aged 25 years'.

The coffin containing Shaw's body, which had meanwhile remained in the church, was afterwards borne to the south-east end of the yard, and placed in a grave not very far distant from those of his relatives. No wreath had been laid on it, and the inscription on the plate was equally simple with that on Wagstaffe's coffin, merely stating his name, the date of his death, and his age (27 years). The duties of the vicar having been fulfilled, the vast concourse of people quietly departed.

It would be interesting to learn what became of James Shaw's family. His wife Mary was left with three sons under five years of age, and through his death James had left them at the mercy of providence.

Mary's grave in the church yard at Christ Church, Stannington, Sheffield

The monumental inscription on the Wagstaffe family gravestone reads:

In Loving Memory of CHARLES
Beloved husband of
ELIZABETH WAGSTAFFE
Born July 20th 1831
Died December 10th 1909
Also MARY ANN, daughter of the above
Also of the above named
ELIZABETH WAGSTAFFE who departed this life June 25th 1921 in
her 90th year
AT REST
Also GEORGE CHARLES son of the above
Died December 15th 1942 Aged 77 years

The memorial is of a later date than Mary's death, and no mention is made of her details. Was the family ashamed by her death? The prevailing view in the late nineteenth century was that suicide was viewed as a shameful act rather than a sin or crime. Whatever their thoughts, her mother Elizabeth, who seems from the newspaper reports to be the main protagonist in ensuring that James and Mary never married, lived another forty years after her daughter's death. Why did she take such a dislike to James? James's memorial is no longer visible.

The execution that the crowds at the funerals were referring to was that of James Hall, aged 53, in Armley Gaol, Leeds. He had murdered his wife.

CHAPTER 16

THE CURSE OF DRINK: THOMAS WHITING, 1882

'In a fit of madness he picked up the child and dashed its head against the dresser'

The *Sheffield and Rotherham Independent* of December 8, 1882 reported details of a terrible incident that had taken place the previous day:

SHOCKING MURDER
IN SHEFFIELD.

A CHILD KILLED BY ITS
FATHER.

Johnson street, a small back lane leading out of the Wicker, was last night the scene of a painful and altogether unexpected drama. At the house No. 40, there lived a man named Thomas Whiting, with his wife and two children, the youngest of whom was an infant, about 14 weeks old.

Also occupying the same house were a man named John Kendall and his wife. Both are steel melters, Whiting being in the employ of Messrs S. Osborn and Co., of the Clyde Steel Works. It is said that he has been rather unsteady, but he was not what could be described as a drunkard, or as one who largely indulged in intoxicating drinks. He was at work on Monday until dinner time, and should have returned yesterday. But instead of doing this he got up at half-past five in the morning, went to the Clyde Steel Works, and said he was not well enough to work. Mrs Whiting noticed that he looked strange on the previous day, and on her asking him yesterday how he was, he said he was 'not right'. On coming back from delivering his message, he went to bed, and there he remained the whole of yesterday. During much of this time his wife was absent, as they had just taken another house, and she was busily occupied in whitewashing the rooms and preparing the place for the furniture. She returned at five o'clock in the evening, and then saw her husband in a chair down stairs, rocking himself backwards and forwards. She asked him if he felt better, and his reply was that he believed he was going off his mind. In consequence of his manner and the strange look in his eyes, she took her eldest child, a little girl, three and a half years old, to her mother's, who lived a short distance off. Some little time afterwards Kendall returned from his work. Whiting was still seated in the chair, and on Kendall remarking that he didn't think he looked right, Whiting said, 'There's summat amiss.' He then talked in a rambling way; so rambling was his language, that Kendall could make nothing of it. Soon afterwards Whiting went up to his bedroom, and Kendall had his tea. The former came down whilst the meal was in progress, sat down for a short time, and then returned to his bedroom. There he remained for a little while, and then once more came downstairs, this time only with his shirt and trousers on. Almost immediately he went up to the cradle in which the infant was sleeping, seized it by the body, and, almost before Kendall was aware of what he was doing, had it out of the cradle. Kendall sprung at once towards him and endeavoured to restrain his violence, but, ere he could do this, Whiting dashed the child's head with great violence on the top of the dresser, and in the struggle which subsequently ensued he threw the child's body towards the fire. The poor mother came in just as this was happening, and picked up the now lifeless body of her child from the fender, and ran with it into a neighbour's house.

Information of what had happened was communicated to Sub-inspector Hill and Police Constable Martin, who were in the Wicker. They at once hurried to Whiting's house, and there found him seated in the room which had just before been the scene of the murder of his child. He was surrounded by several neighbours, and appeared to be tolerably calm. One of them, Mrs Stanley, soon after the occurrence sent for her husband, who was in Stanley Street Chapel, and to him the prisoner, in rather foul language, admitted that he had killed his child. He also said he supposed he would be hanged for it. The police officers conveyed him to the police station in Water Lane, but it was thought useless to formally charge him with the murder of his child, as he appeared out of his mind. He sat down in the charge office till the arrival of Mr Arthur Hallam, the police surgeon, and his assistant. Mr Hallam, after a slight examination of the prisoner, ordered Inspector Bird to watch him, and then went down to Johnson Street to see the child, accompanied by Inspector Hill. His services there could, of course, be of no avail, for the death of the child must have been instantaneous. One side of the skull was battered in.

Two police officers were placed in the cell with Whiting, to see that he did not attempt to destroy himself, and shortly after eleven o'clock Police Sergeant Astill went in with his draught, and endeavoured to coax Whiting to take it. This he at length succeeded in accomplishing, Astill holding the glass in his own hands. Immediately it was removed from his lips Whiting became suddenly exceedingly violent, and made a snatch at it. A struggle thereupon ensued between them, in the course of which Astill got his hand inside the glass and broke it. A portion remained in Whiting's hands, and with this he inflicted a severe wound on Astill's forehead, just above the left eye. There was a smaller wound below the eye. The struggle was heard by Inspector Bird, who was in the charge office below, and assistance was promptly rendered. Subsequently Inspector Bird placed four police officers in the cell, and they remained with Whiting the whole of the night. These were Police Constables Candling, Beech, Pattison, and Parkinson.

The following day another report appeared in the *Sheffield and Rotherham Independent*, describing the unfortunate Whiting's final hours:

THE CHILD MURDER IN SHEFFIELD
DEATH OF THE MURDERER: THE SCENE IN THE CELL
The child murder in Johnson Street, Wicker, on Tuesday night, has had an ending as tragic as it was unexpected. Scarcely more than twelve hours had elapsed from the time that Thomas Whiting, the child's father, killed it in a paroxysm of insanity, ere he, too, was a corpse.

From the time of the murder until his death, Whiting was more or less insane, and during much of it he was a violent and raving maniac. His last hours were of a most terrible description, and the police whose duty it was to spend the night in the cell with Whiting state that a more unpleasant and exhausting time of it they have never experienced since they joined the force. Four officers were placed in his cell with a view of keeping him quiet and of preventing him from doing harm to himself. The task was a most difficult one. The prisoner was a tall, powerfully built man in the prime of life, and the united exertions of the four officers were required to keep him down. Not only did he kick and fight to be free, but his language was of the most horrible description. As one of the officers remarked, 'It made one's flesh creep to hear him.' He frequently made incoherent references to the death of his child, saying, 'I have lost that,' 'I do not care for that,' and so on. At two o'clock yesterday morning the officers were changed, and although those who had left the cell were thoroughly worn out, the prisoner's strength and violence showed no sign of abatement. There could be no question that he was suffering from delirium tremens in its worst form – that he was, in fact, a madman.

When six o'clock came, and with it a relief of the watch, five officers were placed with him – policemen Thompson, Andrews, Allen, Brown, and Vanse – so that some relief might be afforded in turn to those who had to hold the man down, or to go for further assistance if necessary. Throughout the whole of this time the prisoner ceased not in his struggles to be free, and his language became even more wicked and blasphemous than before. At ten o'clock police officers Baker, Semper, Warnock, and Bean took charge of the poor madman, and they had not been long in the cell when they noticed that his struggles became less violent, and that a strange 'rustling' in the throat set in. Sergeant Wynn was informed of the officers' impressions that the beginning of the end had come, and he sent for Mr Hallam, who followed his assistant down almost immediately. Whiting, however, grew gradually worse, and died at twenty minutes to eleven o'clock. Mr Hallam had little doubt that death resulted from acute delirium.

Scarcely any stir was apparent in Johnson Street, yesterday morning, in the neighbourhood of house No.40, where the unfortunate man, with his wife, children and lodgers, lived. At midday it became known that Whiting had died in the cells at the police station, but his wife was not aware of the fact until some little time afterwards, she having left home to transact some business in the office in which her infant's life had been insured. Mrs Whiting is a Sheffield woman, but her husband is said to have been born in India, his father being a soldier, and his mother having accompanied her husband when his regiment was ordered abroad. Whiting's father is believed to be alive now, and residing in America. Mrs Whiting was in great distress Tuesday night, and it can readily be imagined that the news of the death of her husband has increased her grief considerably. The body of the murdered infant is burned and scorched in several parts, but the principal injury has been inflicted on the head, the left side of the skull being battered to a pulp. The body of Whiting lies at the police station to await the coroner's inquest. Last evening that of his child was brought from Johnson Street to the police station, in order that the inquest may take place upon both bodies at the same time. The inquest is fixed for noon to-day.

On December 8 the same newspaper contained two reports on matters relating to the case. The first referred to the condition of Sergeant Astill, who was seriously injured during the repeated attempts by the police to subdue Whiting in the police cells: 'The wound which was inflicted over the left eye of Sergeant Astill on Tuesday night at the police station by the man Thomas Whiting, who was locked up on the charge of murdering his infant daughter, became so painful on Wednesday that he had to remain off duty. Yesterday he became slightly worse and there is, we believe, a danger of erysipelas setting in.' Erysipelas is an acute infection of the skin and underlying fat tissues, usually caused by streptococcus bacteria.

The second report was about the Coroner's inquest. Having heard from several witnesses, including Mrs Whiting, John Kendall (the lodger at No.40 Johnson Street), the police surgeon and some of the policemen directly involved, the Coroner summed up as follows:

[The Coroner remarked] that there were many more witnesses who might be called in this case if the jury considered it necessary. It was the duty of the jury to be satisfied on every point before they attempted to come to a conclusion, and if they considered it desirable they could have before them the policemen who had the care of, and held Thomas Whiting down, almost from the time he entered the cell until his death. The jury, in the exercise of their discretion, would have to consider whether it was necessary to call those constables or not. Under any circumstances they would have to rely very much on the evidence of the medical man, because that gentleman's evidence they were bound to take as unprejudiced, and no one there was in a position to contradict

it. The question was, did the jury consider it necessary to have the evidence of these officers? They acted as his guards. The guard was changed once or twice, and, altogether, a great many policemen had care of him from the time he was taken to the cell until his death. The jury were entitled to hear their evidence, and the law was very jealous indeed about men who died during incarceration, whether in prisons, lunatic asylums, or police cells. Indeed, if there were any suspicion whatever, even the faintest suspicion, well-founded or not, that any form of ill-treatment, violence, or neglect had been practised towards the man during the time he was in the police offices, it would be the duty of the jury to insist upon having the evidence of every person who had anything to do with it. In this case he did not know of any such treatment, and he did not believe there had been any, for it seemed to him that the evidence of the medical man completely passed such a thing to one side. Mr Percy Linley (foreman of the jury) said that the evidence was so conclusive that he thought it was quite unnecessary to call the officers who had charge of Whiting.

The Coroner (continuing) said the cause of the child's death had been explained by the witness Kendall, who was in Whiting's house on Tuesday night. Mr Hallam, the surgeon, said he examined the child, and found that it died from fracture of the skull. He also expressed the opinion that the fracture might have been caused by such injuries as Kendall says he saw Whiting inflict on the child. If they were satisfied with these statements, they could only come to a verdict in accordance with the evidence of Kendall and the surgeon – that would be that Whiting murdered his child. Afterwards they would have to consider what state of mind he was in when he did it. If they thought his mind was affected, and they accepted the facts as proved, their verdict could only be that this child was wilfully murdered by Whiting, he being at that time in an unsound state of mind. As to Whiting's condition, it should not be forgotten that his wife had stated that he had been teetotal until Friday night, and on that night had had little to drink. She also said he was sober on Sunday, and had not much drink on Monday. If that had been the whole of the evidence before the jury as to the state Whiting was really in, it would have left a very serious doubt in their minds, and they would have difficulty in reconciling it with the evidence of the medical man, who said Whiting died from delirium tremens. A fortnight's teetotalism, followed up by a mild and moderate mount of drinking, would not be sufficient to produce delirium tremens. But the woman's evidence was flatly contradicted by Kendall. He swore that

Whiting was drunk on Saturday, fresh on Sunday, and drunk on Monday. The latter was the day before he began to be ill. It was for the jury to decide which of the two were speaking the truth. In deciding the matter the jury were entitled to fall back upon the evidence of the medical man, and Mr Hallam said most positively that the actual cause of death was delirium tremens, and he thought they could come to no other conclusion. After a short deliberation the jury returned the following verdicts:

'That the deceased, Annie Whiting, was wilfully murdered by Thomas Whiting, her father, on the 5th instant, he at the time being of unsound mind and suffering from delirium tremens, brought on by excessive drinking.'

'That the deceased, Thomas Whiting, died on the 6th instant from delirium tremens, brought on by excessive drinking.'

The next day there appeared two sad entries in the 'Births, Marriages and Deaths' column of the *Sheffield and Rotherham Independent*:

Whiting – Dec 5, at 40 Johnson Street, Annie, daughter of Thomas Whiting, aged 14 weeks.

Whiting – Dec 6, at 40 Johnson Street, Thomas Whiting, steel melter, aged 32 years.

The final report from the same newspaper is of the funeral of father and daughter:

THE CHILD MURDER IN SHEFFIELD
FUNERAL OF THE FATHER AND DAUGHTER
On the afternoon of a calm, bright winter's day, and in the presence of a large number of spectators, the remains of Thomas Whiting and of his infant daughter were interred in the Burngreave Cemetery. For some time yesterday afternoon, before that fixed for the funeral, a number of women and children loitered around the door and near the house, and much curiosity was evinced as to whether father and daughter would be enclosed in the same coffin. Shortly before two o'clock a mourning omnibus and a mourning cab drove along the street, and their appearance led the small but orderly crowd at once to come to the conclusion that separate coffins had been provided. The omnibus was first drawn up to the door, and the coffin containing the remains of the father was brought out and placed in the space between the driver's feet. The mourners entered the conveyance, and it was driven a short

distance up the street to make room for that which was to receive the corpse of the child. The sight was a touching one as the little coffin containing the body of the child who had been so cruelly killed, was brought out of the house and placed in the cab. At the side stood two young women dressed in black, with white sashes, white hats and veils. The chief mourners were Mrs Whiting, the widow and mother, who appeared completely overcome as she entered the omnibus; a little girl, Emily Whiting, daughter of the deceased; Mrs Elizabeth Green, Mrs Whiting's mother; Miss Ann Green, her sister; Mrs Ann Moxon, Mr Elijah Moxon, Mr William Bullivant, Mrs Sarah Ann Bullivant, Miss Elizabeth Malone, Mr Charles Green, and Mrs Ann Green. The cortege proceeded by way of Stanley Street into the Wicker, and thence up Spital Hill, and along Burngreave Road, arriving at the cemetery at half-past two o'clock. The afternoon being fine, the number of persons following the two conveyances continued to increase until the cemetery was reached and the coffins carried into the chapel. The burial service was read by the Rev. T. Rigby, of Trinity Church. The grave was situated about 300 yards from the chapel, and on the right-hand side of the central walk. As the mournful procession walked along the path, headed by the clergyman and the bearers carrying the coffins containing husband and daughter, it was not to be wondered that Mrs Whiting was scarcely able to walk, and needed all the assistance her mother, on whose arm she leaned, could afford. Arrived at the graveside, the coffins were lowered to their resting places – that of the child being placed on the lower portion of the coffin which contained the remains of its father.

As the Rev. T. Rigby read the service at the grave side it was pitiful to notice the child Emily, three years of age. She was in the arms of Mr Thomas Hazlehurst, who had served with her father in the army. At her side stood her mother gazing into the grave and weeping bitterly; but the child was filled with wonder, which was pictured in her face as she looked at the vast crowd, then at her sorrowing mother, and at those who were near. When the service was concluded, Mrs Whiting, assisted by her mother, moved forward to take a last look, and as she did so, the tears ran down her cheeks and she sobbed audibly. Scarcely, however, had she moved from the grave side, before she fainted; and two of the men who had borne her husband's body to the grave supported and almost carried her to the outside of the crowd surrounding the grave. The mourners having also taken a last look at the coffins – on the smallest of which a beautiful bouquet of flowers had been thrown – they *left the grave side, and the ceremony concluded. During the service at the grave side there were at least two thousand persons present, who deeply sympathised with the sorrowing widow.*

Grave references for Annie and Thomas Whiting:

Buried on December 10, 1882 in Consecrated Ground; Grave Number 80, Section A6 of Burngreave Cemetery, Sheffield.

Also buried with them is another daughter who died four years earlier:

Whiting, Elizabeth Ann (daughter of Thomas Whiting, age 1). Died at 1-7 Johnson Street; Buried on October 15, 1878 in Consecrated Ground; Grave Number 80, Section A6 of Burngreave Cemetery, Sheffield.

Police Sergeant Astill recovered from his injuries. The 1891 Census showed him living, together with his family, at No.18 Wilson Street, in the Neepsend area of Sheffield, aged 51.

Johnson Street in 2011

CHAPTER 17

PANIC ON GELL STREET, 1883

'The crowd lost its head, and were seized with sudden panic'

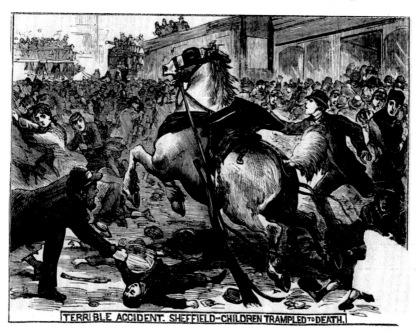

TERRIBLE ACCIDENT. SHEFFIELD—CHILDREN TRAMPLED TO DEATH.

The *Illustrated Police Gazette* of July 14, 1883 carried a report of a tragedy that happened a few days earlier:

SHOCKING ACCIDENT IN SHEFFIELD
TWO KILLED AND SEVERAL INJURED
The procession of the Band of Hope children in Sheffield on Monday was, unfortunately, the cause of an accident, by which two children lost their lives, and several others sustained more or less serious personal injuries. In Gell Street, near the entrance to the depot of the Engineers Corps, was an empty dray belonging to the Midland Railway Company, and in charge of Joseph Johnson, carter. As this afforded an admirable view of the children as they passed along the Glossop Road, the dray was quickly taken possession of by children and grown-up persons. Johnson at first endeavoured to prevent this, but the crowd were too many for him, and at length he gave up the task in despair. The dray then became crowded, children for the most part standing at the front, whilst men and women stood at the back. All round the vehicle there was a compact mass of spectators.

The horse stood quietly enough until the highly decorated wagon of the Hanover Chapel Band of Hope came in sight. Then the spectators cheered, and it is said the horse became restive at the noise. Another version is that in their eagerness to see the design, some of those who were standing at the back of the dray pushed forward, the effect being to force some of the children in front upon the animal's back and hind legs. Whatever the cause, the horse plunged, and then made its way towards Glossop Road. There was instantly a scene of the wildest excitement and confusion. As the dray went swaying along, the children were jolted out on either side, and fell struggling and screaming to the ground, where they were trodden upon by those who were near. Had the crowd remained quiet probably no lives would have been sacrificed. But consisting as it did largely of women and children, the crowd lost its head, and were seized with sudden panic. In their eagerness to get out of the way of the horse they surged backwards and forwards, with the inevitable result that the weakest were thrown down, and lay at the mercy of those above them.

The cries of the injured attracted the attention of Police Constable Needham, who had been stationed in Glossop Road to prevent persons from entering Mr H. M. Shera's garden, and he endeavoured to make his way to the scene. This was a work of much difficulty, in consequence of the excited condition of the crowd, and he states that for several minutes he was scarcely able to keep his legs. In the meantime the horse had liberated itself from the harness and made its way towards the Glossop Road. There it was stopped, and prevented from doing further mischief. Needham first directed his efforts to restoring something like order amongst the crowd, and when this was happily accomplished he and others attended to those who were the most seriously injured. Cabs were procured for the worst cases, and they were taken as quickly as possible to the hospital. Others were carried there by friends and relatives. One child, John Charles Summers, two years of age, was dead when he was picked up. The poor little thing was lying at the bottom of a heap of struggling humanity, and from the fact that the body presented no external marks of violence the supposition is that its death was caused by suffocation, Another child, who was lying near, died almost immediately after his admission into the hospital. This was Frederick Lawless, four years of age. Several who were taken to the hospital or who walked there were not seriously injured and left the institution as soon as their wounds were dressed. Others, who were more seriously injured, remained a few hours.

The following is the list of the killed: Frederick Lawless, four years, No.7 Sarah Street. John Charles Summers, two years, No.2 Jericho Street. Injured: Emma Lawless, 39 years, Sarah Street, fractured skull and fractured legs; Ben Lawless, Sarah Street, severe internal injuries; Minnie Laud, Blake Street, scalp wound and other injuries; Henry Taylor, No.5 Court, Gilbert Street, injury to leg and contusions; Mary Ann Bellamy, 25 years, Martin Street, contused bruises; John Britson, No.57 St Stephen's Road, contusions of shoulder and other injuries; Charles Hatfield, Flat Street, contusions of leg; Sarah Norman, 37 years, injury to chest and internal injuries; Annie Dawson, 18 years, Hoyle Street, injury to her knee; Hannah England, 45 years, No.15 Court, Gilpin Street, bruised and shaken; John William Steel, child, Creswick Street, bruised and shaken; Mrs Bishop, Mowbray Street, knocked down and trampled upon.

On Wednesday an inquest was held at the hospital, before Mr D. Wightman, touching the death of two children. In answer to the Coroner, Mr Wilson said Mr Beal, of the firm of Messrs Beal and Marigold, solicitors to the Midland Railway Company, would probably represent the company if the inquiry were adjourned. The Coroner, addressing the jury, said: 'In this case, as you are probably aware, we are met to inquire as to the cause of death of those two children, who have died from injuries received on Monday. I understand that it will be necessary to adjourn the inquiry. For some reason or other, the Midland Railway Company, the owners of the dray, which, whether it caused the accident or not I am not prepared to say, but at any rate, it is supposed in some shape or way to have contributed to it, are anxious that their solicitor should be present.

The jury having viewed the bodies, the witness called was Thomas Lee Lawless, wire drawer, of No.7 Sarah Street, father of the deceased, Frederick Lawless. He said he last saw the deceased alive on Sunday night. He was at work when the accident happened. About half past six he went to the hospital, where he found his child dead. Elizabeth Summers, wife of Charles Summers, spring-knife cutler, No.12 Court, Jericho Street, identified the other child, and said he was killed on Monday last, but she was not present when the accident occurred.

The scene of the accident: the junction of Gell Street and Glossop Road (photograph 2011)

The inquest was adjourned, resuming the following day, and was reported in the *Sheffield and Rotherham Independent*:

Harriet Smith, wife of Joseph Smith, of Jericho Street, said she was with the child Summers, in Gell Street, when the Band of Hope procession was passing along Glossop Road. She was on the road with the deceased. There was a great crowd. A horse and dray were standing by, and on the dray were many young men and women. She saw a little boy hit the horse on the nose with his hand, and she told him not to do so. A young man put his arm on the shaft, and the horse gave a kind of 'chink'. She had the child Summers in her arms, and was knocked down by the dray, and she did not remember anything further until some time afterwards.

The driver of the dray, Joseph Johnson, was then called:

He said he was a drayman in the employ of the Midland Railway Company, and about two o'clock on the afternoon of the 2nd inst. He drove from Portobello Street down Gell Street to see the procession. He pulled his horse up about 30 yards from the Glossop Road crossing, locked the wheel, and took the collar or 'hame' chain off the horse. People began getting on the dray to obtain a better view of the procession. He tried to keep them off, but could not. He then stood about a couple of yards in front of his horse, leaving his lad Arthur Rogers in charge of it. All went well until the people began clapping their hands as the gaily-dressed Hanover Street wagon passed. There was some commotion, and when he turned round his horse was just leaving the shafts. The animal went at a sharpish pace towards Glossop Road, but afterwards walked, and was stopped by a young man. There was another dray standing between his horse and Glossop Road. Neither of the drays turned right over, but when his horse drew forward the lighter dray standing nearer Glossop Road might be lifted up a little. He could not say what else occurred, for he was too much occupied in looking after his mare. He did not see either of the deceased children injured or carried away. His mare was one of the quietest animals in Sheffield. It was his opinion that she was startled by some of the children being pushed off the dray on to her hocks. The witness, continuing, said his lad Rogers was seriously hurt about the legs by the crowd.

Arthur Rogers was carried into the room, and examined by the Coroner. He gave his evidence in a very straightforward way. He said he was standing by the horse's head when the accident occurred. He thought the clapping and applause as the Hanover Street wagon passed frightened the horse, and caused it to plunge. He was knocked down by the crowd when the horse broke out of the shafts, and lay face downwards. He felt something go over him, but could not say what. He was hurt in the side and leg. He did not see Johnson after the dray was drawn up, but he kept near the horse. It was a very quiet animal, and he did not think it would shy. He could manage it very well – indeed he took it to and from the stable every day, and it never gave him any trouble.

The Coroner said the evidence throughout the inquest was of a very indefinite character. The only question which had occurred to him throughout the whole course of the inquiry was whether the conduct of the man Johnson had been satisfactorily explained. Had he acted wisely in leaving the horse's head? The mare would not shy at traction engines, and the boy considered himself capable of attending to her, and he had charge of her when the accident occurred. When the rush took place the lad had no strength either to contend with the crowd or the horse, and he was knocked down and trampled upon.

The jury at once returned a verdict 'That the deceased were accidentally killed on the 2nd inst., probably by being crushed or trod upon in a crowd, while watching a procession of the Bands of Hope'.

Lawless, the father of one of the deceased children, thought Johnson should be censured for leaving the dray. The jury and the Coroner expressed a different opinion, and the proceedings terminated.

A verdict of accidental death was probably appropriate in this case, despite the protestations of the father of one of the dead children, as nobody could have foreseen that the horse would be frightened by the noise created by a great number of people.

Regarding the residences of the victims, Sarah Street has been obliterated by road widening and the creation of the Brook Hill roundabout. It ran down the hill parallel to St Philip's Road. Jericho Street still exists, but in much truncated form compared with its past existence. It runs opposite Hammond Street and abuts Netherthorpe Road, the dual carriageway that runs down from Brook Hill roundabout to Shalesmoor. It used to continue all the way to Upper Allen Street. Gell Street was probably named after Sir John Gell, of Hopton, Derbyshire, who, during the Civil War, took Sheffield town and castle for the Parliamentarians on October 11, 1642.

Jericho Street in 2011

CHAPTER 18

WHO KILLED THE BEARDED LADY?
BODEN LANE, 1883

'The man obtained celebrity in country fairs as "The Bearded Lady"'

In Sheffield's City Road Cemetery, there is the grave of a William Ratcliffe, which he shares with eight other interments. The record of William's burial states:

> *Ratcliffe, William (scale presser, age 45); Died at Boden Lane; Buried on October 12, 1883 in Consecrated Ground. Grave Number 11917, Section X of City Road Cemetery, Sheffield.*

A report in the *Sheffield and Rotherham Independent* on October 13, 1883 explained how William died:

> SUSPICIOUS DEATH OF THE
> "BEARDED LADY."
>
> A man who for a number of years travelled about the country and was shown at fairs as "The Bearded Lady," has met with his death in a shocking manner, in the house which he occupied, situate in a miserable-looking court off Rockingham street.

His real name was William Ratcliffe, but he was chiefly known as 'Poll', or by the title which he bore when being exhibited by a showman. Probably it was his small face, thin long hands, and effeminate mode of speech which caused him to appear in public as a female, and there can be no doubt that he used at one time to go about in the streets impersonating a female. About five months ago he rented a house in No.1 court, Boden Lane, and this he has since occupied by himself. His effeminate demeanour, combined with a knowledge of his having previously moved about as a woman, and of his living a peculiar existence, caused him to be a well-known character in some of the low parts of the town. He had learnt one of the Sheffield handicrafts, but since he took to housekeeping he has eked out an existence by gathering and selling herbs and telling fortunes in public houses. His vaunted powers as a herbalist and a fortune-teller do not appear to have caused him to be feared like the witches of old were by the lower classes, but he has been an object of scorn and banter to may roughs on account of his womanish ways. Altogether he was a most extraordinary character, and just as his career was so singular so is his death shocking.

The court in which he resided is about one of the worst of its class in the town. The deceased frequently visited Wallace's vaults in Campo Lane, but sometimes he had not the wherewithal to purchase a glass of beer, and the landlord would then allow him to sit down, and not infrequently gave him a glass of liquor. On Saturday night he entered Wallace's vaults, went briskly up to the singing room, and, having spoken a word or two with the landlady, descended into the bar. He seemed in a lively mood, and stayed there some time, during which he had a couple of glasses of beer, paid for by a friend named Thomas Parkin. About half-past nine they went together to the Paradise vaults close by, where they had more beer. It was the deceased's habit to go home before eleven o'clock, for he appears to have been afraid of walking along late by himself, lest he should be set on by some of the roughs who infest the neighbourhood. Between a quarter and half-past twelve Mrs Darwint, a neighbour, heard the deceased exclaim, 'Oh, poor Poll,' but she did not conceive anything was wrong. There was no disturbance, and it is not imagined a great struggle took place. Mr Darwint had engaged to go, on Sunday morning, to Askham's works near by to clean out the engine and boiler, and as he was leaving his house about six o'clock he perceived a cat in the yard. The animal made a horrible noise, and he ran towards it. The cat descended to *near the deceased's house, and he followed. To his surprise he noticed that the door was open, and fearing something was wrong, he looked inside. He then saw the deceased lying on the floor, with his face downwards, and in a pool of blood. He was unconscious, and Darwint at once created an alarm, with the result that several neighbours came in. Later on Mr Skinner, surgeon, of Brookhill, the 'parish doctor', visited the house, but the condition of the deceased had not changed, and Mr Skinner could render him little assistance. Shortly after eight o'clock on Monday morning he again saw the deceased, who was still unconscious, and about half-past nine Ratcliffe expired.*

Ratcliffe was a native of Sheffield, and was taught the trade of a burnisher. His father, after much saving, gave him, when a young man, a sum of £10 to forward his prospects, and he continued to work steadily until he married a woman possessed of about £20, when he grew idle. He squandered the money, they separated, and then it was that he took to appearing as a woman. It is believed that his wife went to America, and is still living. His relatives, however, were so ashamed of his conduct that they ceased to hold intercourse with him, and an elder brother who on viewing the corpse informed our representative that he knew little in regard to him, not having spoken to him for several years.

An inquest took place soon afterwards, reported in detail in the *Sheffield and Rotherham Independent*:

The inquiry into the circumstances attending the death of William Ratcliffe, was opened on Wednesday at the George and Dragon Hotel, Broad Lane, before Mr Dossy Wightman, the Coroner. The Coroner said he would take the medical evidence first, and Mr William Skinner, surgeon, Brookhill, was sworn. He said he had attended the deceased some months ago. The man told him he was better after he had seen him several times, and he ceased to attend him. He saw him last on Sunday night. About eight o'clock he received a Union order for attendance on the deceased. He saw the deceased about a quarter past eight o'clock. He was then alive, and on the floor of the house where he lived. He was perfectly unconscious. He saw the deceased again on the Monday morning a little before nine o'clock. He was dying then. He was not present at his death. He had made a post-mortem examination on the man. Outwardly he found a severe bruise over the left eye. The deceased was bleeding from the nose and eye. He was bleeding from these organs when he saw him on Sunday night. The bruise over the eye was contused; the skin was not broken. There were no other outward marks of violence. Internally he found a most extensive fracture of the skull, over the roof of the left eye and the nose to the base of the skull. The brain was flooded with blood. The ventricles of the brain were full of clots, and the membranes were distended with blood.

The Coroner: 'How were his internal organs?'

Witness: 'There was congestion of the stomach. Extravation of blood from the fracture in the head was the cause of death.'

The Coroner: 'Might this injury have been caused by a fall?'

Witness: 'I don't think the deceased could have been injured to such an extent in that way by any possibility.'

Thomas Parkin, of No.7 court, Thomas Street, table-knife handle presser, said he had known the deceased a long time by sight, but to speak to perhaps three months. He had seen him infrequently until ten weeks ago, when witness left the town. He returned on the 2nd inst., and saw the deceased the same night at the Paradise Inn, Paradise Street. The deceased was in the habit of visiting that house.

Parkin explained that he and Ratcliffe had been out together on Saturday night. Ratcliffe was not the worse for drink and there had been no quarrelling with anyone. They met at the Haven Hotel, at the top of Fitzwilliam Street, then had a walk round town and called at the Paradise Inn, where they stayed from eight o'clock to half-past-nine. They then had another walk, this time through the market, calling at the Pitcher and Glass, or Virginia Vaults, in Paradise Street. There they remained until eleven o'clock.

The Coroner: 'Did you go home with him?'

Witness: 'I went as far as St Thomas Street, in Portobello, with him.'

'Do you mean to say he went home alone?'

'He went on St Thomas Street towards home, and I on Orange Street. I can't say that he went home.'

Witness had no suspicion as to who had caused the deceased's injuries, and had not the slightest idea of anyone likely to hurt him. The deceased had no money on him excepting three halfpence, which witness gave him to get a glass of beer with. He did not spend this money in witness's presence, however, and would probably have it on him when he went home.

The next witness called was Frederick Darwint, of No.3 house, No.1 court, Boden Lane, who described how he found Ratcliffe lying badly injured early on Sunday morning. He said Ratcliffe's head and arms were outside the house, the rest of his body inside, with the door wide open. He was dressed, and alive, but unconscious. He was bleeding a little and appeared to have vomited. Darwint called out to his neighbour, Mr Richardson, to help him get Ratcliffe inside the house. However, there was a man in the yard, whom Darwint did not recognise and who, he said, appeared to have been there all night. The man told Darwint that Richardson was in bed, so Darwint went to his house and called from the bottom of the stairs. This time Richardson heard him, came down to help and the pair carried Ratcliffe inside the house and placed him near the fireplace. The Coroner asked witness how far away from Ratcliffe he lived.

'About twenty yards.'

'What time did you get home Saturday night?'

'Just after eight o'clock.'

'Did you hear any noise during the night?'

'Only once, when I heard Ratcliffe give an alarm, which he has done before to get me out of bed.'

'What did he say?'

'Oh, dear, poor Poll.'

'You say it was nothing unusual for him to cry out in the night?

'He has done so frequently in order to alarm me.'

'Why you specially?'

'Only for fun, and that has put me on my guard. Had he not done it before I should have run at once to him.'

Darwint believed he was the first to find the unconscious man – the first to acknowledge he had found him anyway. He added that if someone else had found Ratcliffe first it was a wrong affair for that person to do nothing, as they must have heard his groans, which Darwint heard as soon as he got up. He said there was a cat on the opposite wall, 'shrieking like a tiger and setting itself at Ratcliffe', seemingly very frightened. He had to drive the cat away. He added that if there had been any quarrel in Ratcliffe's house during the night he would have heard it as he was a light sleeper. When he found Ratcliffe there were no implements lying around that could obviously have been used to strike him. The only thing he could think of for somebody attacking Ratcliffe was that some unknown person had a grievance with him. At this point the Coroner adjourned the inquest, saying that the police officers present had heard what had been said, and the surprise expressed by the last witness that the stranger in the yard had not found the deceased. That was sufficient to give the police a clue, and they had better let the matter remain where it was for the present pending further enquiries.

The inquest was re-opened on October 19, 1883. A report the next day gave brief details of the conclusions reached:

> *The Sheffield coroner yesterday resumed the inquest on the body of William Ratcliffe of Boden Lane, Sheffield, who obtained celebrity in country fairs as 'The Bearded Lady'. His death occurred on the 8th inst. in mysterious circumstances. He was found lying across the threshold of his house in an unconscious state, and an examination proved that his skull was fractured seriously. The doctor who made the post-mortem examination gave it as his opinion that the wound could only have been caused by a very severe blow, and he thought that it highly improbable that it had been accidentally inflicted. Nothing further was discovered, and an open verdict was recorded.*

The medical examiner was certain that death was not accidental, yet an open verdict was recorded. It is highly probable that William was murdered by a person or persons unknown, but given that he was 'wretchedly poor', the impression remains that it was deemed prudent to return an open verdict rather than have an unsolved murder on the books. The police no doubt did make enquiries but these would have been of a cursory nature, and once they had been unsuccessfully completed, they would not have wanted to devote any additional resources to apprehending William's murderer. The motive was unlikely to have been robbery, as William had little in the way of possessions and, according to Thomas Parkin, only three halfpence in money. Unable to afford a grave of his own, poor William was buried in a joint interment. William's hovel disappeared many years ago – it was located in one of Sheffield's most notorious slum areas. But Boden Lane still exists today, running between Rockingham Street and Bailey Lane, near their junction with Broad Lane.

The internet encyclopaedia 'Wikipedia' describes the phenomenon of 'The Bearded Lady' thus:

> *A bearded lady or bearded woman is a woman who has a visible beard. These women have long been a phenomenon of legend, curiosity,*

ridicule, and more recently, political statement and fashion statement. A small number of women are able to grow enough facial hair to have a distinct beard. In some cases, female beard growth is the result of a hormonal imbalance (usually androgen excess), or a rare genetic disorder known as hypertrichosis. Notable exceptions were the famous (and usually fake) bearded women of the circus sideshows of the 19th and early 20th centuries, before so-called freak shows became unpopular.

William Ratcliffe must have been one of the 'fake bearded women of the circus sideshows', as it was explained at the inquest that he was a man who happened to have a small face and long, slender hands, an effeminate voice and manner and who was known to sometimes dress as a woman. No mention was made of his having any other female characteristics; or perhaps, if he did, it would have been taboo to mention it.

Boden Lane, Sheffield (photograph 2011)

CHAPTER 19

MULTIPLE MURDERS AT WHITE CROFT, 1884

'Don't do it to me, dada'

The Times of July 11, 1884 gave an account of a multiple murder that occurred in White Croft, a narrow lane near the centre of Sheffield, the previous day. White Croft lay within an area called the Crofts, which was a slum district of Sheffield comprising tightly-packed houses and small workshops. It stood in the area below Hawley Street and down to West Bar and Shalesmoor. Much of it was cleared from the late 1890s onwards, but White Croft still exists, running uphill off Tenter Street, towards Solly Street.

MURDERS IN SHEFFIELD.

A shocking affair occurred in Sheffield yesterday morning. In a house in No. 2 Court, Whitecroft, lived a man named Joseph Laycock, with his wife, Maria Laycock, and four children—Sarah, aged eight years; Frank, aged six; Mary, aged four; and Joseph, two years old.

Laycock was a hawker, but he was idle and dissolute, and followed his calling very fitfully. About Whitsuntide he got into trouble with the police, to whom he was well known, and was sentenced to 21 days' imprisonment. He was released on Saturday, and on the evening of that day there was a quarrel between him and his wife, and he threatened to 'do for her'. On Thursday night the two were drinking together in some public house. They left for home shortly before 11 o'clock, and were then friendly with each other. About midnight, however, a little girl heard Mrs Laycock utter a fearful scream inside the house, and later two young men heard Laycock walking about the Croft in an agitated state. Yesterday morning the neighbours were surprised to find that Laycock's door remained shut and that no one was moving within. At 10 o'clock three women living in the court tried the door, pushed it open, and discovered what had taken place during the night. Mrs Laycock was lying on the floor in a pool of blood, her head nearly severed from her body. Mrs Kidnew, one of the neighbours, proceeded upstairs, and saw the feet of Laycock behind the door. His legs moved, and Mrs Kidnew, afraid of his violence, ran downstairs without making further search. It was at first thought that the four children were safe at the house of their grandmother. When this was found not to be the case the excitement became very great. Sergeant Hornsey was called from a neighbouring police station, and he was the first to ascertain the actual condition of things upstairs. Laycock was lying on a mattress behind the door with a severe gash in his throat. He was just able to speak, and said to the officer, whom he well knew, 'Bob, let me die, don't move me; let me die.' Hornsey cast his eye round the room and saw the four children lying on the floor with their throats cut, and all dead and cold. Three were lying together on one mattress, and the fourth on another mattress near Laycock. By the side of the murderer was a bread knife, with which, no doubt, the murders had been committed.

Laycock was immediately conveyed to the hospital in West Street, where his wound was dressed. Though he has suffered great loss of blood, the belief is entertained that he will recover. It seems certain that the injury to himself was not inflicted until several hours after the murders. The body of Mrs Laycock was downstairs, fully dressed, proving that she was killed before going to bed, and all the bodies were cold and stiff. The condition of the house as regards furniture was pitiable. Beyond a three-legged table, a couple of chairs, a cradle, a lamp, and a little crockery, the house was bare of contents. Mrs Laycock, though she occasionally gave way to drink, was a hard-working woman, who endeavoured to provide for her children.

The inquest was opened yesterday afternoon at the public mortuary, whither the bodies were removed. It was stated that no date could be fixed for the appearance of the prisoner, who, though he has inflicted a

106

bad wound on himself, had not injured any vital part. Last night he made a statement to the house surgeon at the hospital admitting he committed the murders. He said that both he and his wife went home drunk together, that the woman said she wished she was dead, and that he then lost his senses and committed the murders. He first cut the throat of his wife, who did not offer any resistance, and then he went upstairs and cut the throats of three of his children. Afterwards he took the youngest on his knee. The child said, 'Don't do it to me, dada,' but he cut his throat and then his own.

MURDER OF A WIFE AND FOUR CHILDREN AT SHEFFIELD.

An illustration of the scene of the murders from the Illustrated Police News

A few days later the *Western Mail* reported:

THE HORRIBLE MURDERS AT SHEFFIELD

The man Joseph Laycock who murdered his wife and four children at Sheffield and then cut his own throat is progressing towards recovery. He has a terrible wound on his throat, but none of his main arteries were severed. Though in a state of great excitement for several hours after his admission to the hospital, he is calm now and talks of the certainty of the fate that awaits him. He does not seem to be aware why he committed the murders except that he and his wife quarrelled. They were both the worse for drink. The funeral of Maria Laycock and her four children murdered by Joseph Laycock at Sheffield last Friday took place at Intake Cemetery near Sheffield on Monday. There were about 30,000 present.

The *Manchester Guardian* described the remarkable scenes at the funeral in more detail:

The mother and four children murdered last Friday at Sheffield by Laycock, the hawker, were interred on Monday afternoon at the Intake Cemetery, just outside the town, the Rev. A. R. Shaw officiating. An immense number of people gathered to see interment, there being no less than 25,000 people at the cemetery. The crushing was fearful, and many women fainted, but at the grave order was kept by a large body of police.

This must have been one of the largest gatherings for a funeral in the history of Sheffield. The funeral took place on July 14, 1884. The five coffins were loaded into a mourning coach that had been purchased by public subscription. The cortège made its way along Millsands, Blonk Street, Furnival Road, Broad Street and Duke Street on its way to Intake Cemetery (now known as City Road Cemetery). Thousands lined the route, many of them continuing on to the cemetery. Police had difficulty controlling the crowds as the five bodies were laid to rest in a single grave in the paupers' section of the cemetery. The coffins of the children were carried to their final resting place by their friends. They were buried in the same grave, reference 11894, section X, City Road.

Maria Laycock and her family's last resting place

A report of Laycock's trial appeared in *The Times* on August 6, 1884:

At Leeds yesterday, before Mr Justice Mathew, Joseph Laycock, hawker, was charged with murder of his daughter Sarah Ann Laycock at Sheffield on the 10th of July. Mr Fenwick and Mr C. M. Atkinson conducted the prosecution; and the prisoner was defended by Mr Meysey-Thompson. The prisoner, on being brought up for trial, seemed to be in a prostrate condition. For some time he cried bitterly, and apparently felt his condition acutely. During the progress of the trial he gradually became calmer, but throughout the proceedings he kept his head buried in his hands. The details of the case were of a terrible character. The prisoner lived with his wife Maria Laycock in Sheffield. They had four children – Sarah Ann aged eight years; Francis George aged six years; Mary Ann aged four years and Joseph aged two years. At about 6 o'clock on the above day the prisoner saw a police constable and made some complaint to him about his wife drinking with another man. He was perfectly sober at this time. At 10 o'clock the prisoner and his wife were having some supper together. He asked her to have some drink, and upon her refusing to take any he said, 'You might as well have some while you have the chance; it will be the last time you have the chance.' They afterwards went home quietly together. In the middle of the night a scream was heard, and upon the prisoner's house being entered a horrible sight presented itself. The body of his wife was found on the floor in the kitchen. Her throat was cut and she was quite dead. The bodies of all the children were found on the floor in a bed room upstairs. Their throats had been cut and they were all dead. The prisoner was also lying on the floor in the bed room, and close to his hand there was a large table knife covered in blood. His own throat was also cut.

A man named Pearson said to him, 'Good God, what have you done?' He made no reply but put his hands to his lips as if in the act of prayer. The prisoner was at once taken to the hospital. Whilst being attended to he said to the surgeon, 'Let me die' and 'cut my throat deeper.' He was taken into custody on the 25th of July and upon being charged with murdering his wife and four children he said, 'It was all through drink; it was about midnight when I did it.' The prisoner was said to have been very good to and fond of his children, but to have been in trouble several times for assaults. The facts were undisputed, and the only defence set up was that the prisoner was not at the time responsible for his acts. To support this contention several witnesses were called on his behalf, and from their evidence it was shown that for some days previously to the 10th of July the prisoner had appeared very strange.

Until he was seven years old he suffered from an affection in his head for which he was attended by a medical man. His grandfather on his mother's side and his father were both found drowned and two brothers of his mother committed suicide, the one by cutting his throat, and the other by throwing himself before an engine. The prisoner was also apparently subject to delusions. The surgeon of the hospital in Sheffield to which the prisoner was taken gave evidence tending to show that he was not responsible for acts at the time he committed the crime with which he was charged.

The learned judge, in summing up the case to the jury said that when he first looked at the depositions he came to the conclusion that it would not be right that the case should go to the jury upon the bare evidence the prosecution proposed to bring forward; he had therefore asked learned counsel to undertake the defence and to obtain the services of some professional gentleman who would be able to make inquiries into the previous history of the prisoner and as to his mental condition. With regard to the case itself, his Lordship said that the very atrocity of the crime itself rather suggested that it was not the act of a sane man and the jury would probably think that there was insanity in the prisoner's family at all events. The jury retired to consider their verdict and returning into the court after a short absence found the prisoner 'Guilty', and he was sentenced to death in the usual form. After the sentence the prisoner remained clasping the rail of the dock with both hands. Two warders removed his hands with a little force. The prisoner then exclaimed to the Judge, who had risen, 'Thank you your Worship, thank you.' He was then led by the warders down the steps.

Joseph Laycock had spent all his life in and out of work, first as an errand boy, then as a pot moulder, and then as a hand in a rolling mill. During this time he had acquired a string of convictions for petty crime, mostly involving theft and drunkenness. There was also a violent side to him: in 1879 he was arrested on suspicion of stabbing a man and had a local reputation as a prize fighter. He married Maria on May 16, 1875, at St Philip's Church, Shalesmoor but, according to Maria's mother, the marriage was unhappy from the beginning. There were frequent rows that often culminated in violence. On two occasions Joseph had actually tried to kill Maria. In June 1884 he was sentenced to 21 days' imprisonment for assaulting and beating her but the sentence had no deterrent effect because within a day of being released there were more disturbances. According to the neighbours and family the cause of the violence was the potent combination of jealousy and drink. Maria was a habitual drinker who would fly into violent fits of rage when confronted with the consequences of her drinking. Joseph's 'excuse' for his conduct was that he was trying to break his wife's drinking habits but as his court convictions show he was not averse to drinking himself into a stupor. The house in White Croft where the family was living in July 1884 is described in David Bentley's book *Sheffield Murders 1865-1965* thus:

> *A more squalid poverty-stricken abode [could not] be imagined. Situated at the right-hand corner of the entrance to the Croft [the house had] one [room] on the ground floor and two upstairs… had scarcely a stick of furniture and [conveyed] the impression of having existed innumerable years in perfect innocence of soap and water.*

Maria Laycock spent her final morning collecting spent medicine bottles to earn extra money, but after midday she started drinking. She was accosted in the late afternoon by her mother at the Warm Hearthstone Inn in Townhead Street. Her mother accused her of spending money on drink whilst her children were suffering neglect and hunger. On hearing this, the landlord refused to serve Maria and threw her out. She was next seen fighting with a woman in Hawley Croft and at six o'clock a witness saw her husband fetching Maria from another pub. This resulted in a street fight between the couple. A policeman walked by and Laycock shouted: 'She's been drinking with another man. Take her in and me an' all.' The police told them to go home. Joseph did so, but Maria went to her mother's and together with her brother Christopher set off for Glossop Road to sell the medicine bottles they had collected. On the way back it rained heavily, so Maria and Christopher stopped at the Bearders public house in Pea Croft for a drink. On leaving the pub, Maria met her husband and yet another quarrel started. This time Maria ran off. However, by ten o'clock the couple were seen drinking together in the Rawson's Arms in Tenter Street, where they also ate supper. They left shortly before eleven o'clock and returned home. A row soon developed but as it was a common occurrence, the neighbours ignored it. At midnight a woman's scream was heard. And then there was silence.

Throughout his trial Laycock expressed remorse, sobbing bitterly and begging for forgiveness. He was sent for execution at Armley Gaol in Leeds. In a death-cell statement Laycock blamed his mother-in-law for the tragedy. He said she took her daughter out drinking and she would then often return home unfit to look after either him or the children. On the night of the murders he had resolved to kill himself and went to kiss the children for the last time. When he went downstairs his wife had goaded and taunted him, and that is when he was overcome by madness.

The execution of Laycock was notable was several reasons. The authorities refused to admit the press, the rumours being that there had been a number of botched executions recently at Leeds. Laycock was due to be hanged by a new hangman, James Billington, and they were apparently fearful of another fiasco. The scaffold in the prison yard at Armley Gaol was the same one used to hang one of Sheffield's most infamous criminals, Charles Peace, in 1876. The *Daily News* of August 26, 1884 reported that Laycock was calm and resigned to his fate on the eve of his execution, but it on the day his 'courage and fortitude' deserted him. Laycock fainted in the cell and had to be escorted to the scaffold. He was reported to have asked, just before being hanged: 'You will not hurt me?' to which Billington replied: 'No, tha'll nivver feel it, for tha'll be out of existence i' two minutes.' As the noose was being tightened around his neck, Laycock exclaimed: 'Oh my children, my children. Lord have mercy on my children.' He was then dispatched into oblivion. His crime remains Sheffield's worst-ever mass murder.

In October 2007 Chris Hobbs was contacted by a descendent of Maria Laycock. The respondent was researching her family's history and in the course of her investigations realised that the victims of the murder were her ancestors. She wrote: 'Christopher Green was my great grandfather and Maria Laycock was my great-great aunt. Christopher and Maria were related through the same mother but different fathers. Very little is known about them as Christopher and his wife Louisa committed suicide in 1900, orphaning their children. My grandfather and his brother and sisters apparently never spoke of their parents. Though the story of Maria and her children's death is tragic, it at least gives some insight into what the situation for my ancestors was in the 1880s. Maria's maiden name was either Connor or O'Connor, but I had lost track of her after the 1871 Census. I had found Maria Connor in the 1861 Census as a two-year-old, living with her 22-year-old widowed mother and a family named Kelly. The address seems to read Lambert Street. Her mother was Ann Connor, whose place of birth was Huddersfield. Maria was born in Sheffield on October 21, 1861. Ann Connor (formerly White) married John Green at St Philip's Church. The description of the family living at White Croft and the subsequent suicides paints a picture of a rather dysfunctional family, which makes it all the more impressive that the surviving children (my grandfather and great aunts and great uncle) actually did well for themselves and raised children who for the most part succeeded in life. Maria Laycock's mother, my great-great grandmother, Ann Green, also committed suicide at No.17 Scargill Croft on December, 7, 1900 by "taking spirits of salt during a state of temporary insanity". Christopher and Maria's youngest brother Henry

Green also committed suicide in February 1901 at Scargill Croft, by taking poison presumed to be hydrochloric acid.'

Two views of White Croft: around 1900 (top, courtesy Sheffield Local Studies Library) and 2012 (bottom)

CHAPTER 20

A FATAL QUARREL, THE MOOR, 1886

'Are you going to murder me or what do you want?'

The following report appeared in *The Times* on January 12, 1886 and related to a court case that occurred the previous day at Sheffield Town Hall:

A FATAL QUARREL.—At Sheffield Town-hall yesterday, before the Stipendiary, James Eaton, 17, hammer grinder, was charged with the manslaughter of Harvey Bell, 22, a journeyman butcher, on January 2.

The prisoner was acting as chairman in the singing room of the Woodman Inn, Sheffield Moor. Bell and other persons were present. Eaton accused a man named Dodworth of interrupting the music by making a noise. Dodworth denied this, and a quarrel afterwards took place outside the public house, in which Bell got mixed up. Eaton, it is alleged, felled Bell to the ground, thrashed Dodworth, and then attacked Bell again, striking him fiercely in the face and knocking him down a second time. Though able to go home, Bell experienced great pain next day, and was taken to the hospital, where he became unconscious, and died from a fractured skull. The prisoner was committed for trial at the Leeds Assizes, the defence being reserved.

Eaton was a hammer grinder and lived at Saxon Road, Heeley, whilst Bell lived at No.60 Napier Street, Sharrow. Eaton, initially charged with inflicting grievous bodily harm, saw his charge upgraded to manslaughter after Bell's death. Eaton's father applied for bail, but it was denied. The *Sheffield and Rotherham Independent* reported the case:

ALLEGED MANSLAUGHTER IN SHEFFIELD
The unfortunate man, Harvey Bell, who was knocked down and injured in a scuffle in Young Street, Sheffield Moor, on Wednesday night, died about five o'clock yesterday. By this melancholy termination to his sufferings, the charge against James Eaton, who was in custody charged with inflicting grievous bodily harm, has been converted to one of manslaughter, upon which he was yesterday brought up at the Town Hall, before Mr J. H. Barber and Ald. W. H. Brittain, and remanded till Monday next. The affair was a deplorable termination to a public house musical evening, the man in custody being chairman of a singing meeting held at the Woodman Inn, Sheffield Moor. Some unpleasantness occurred during the evening between the chairman, Eaton, and a man named Dodworth, as a result of which there was a challenge to fight, and a fight was arranged to take place between Eaton and Dodworth. The latter, however, left the house by a back way leading into Young Street. Subsequently, Eaton and several others, amongst them the deceased, Harvey Bell, left the house by the front door, and they were standing by the door talking, when, it is alleged, that Eaton struck deceased a violent blow in the face, causing him to stagger and fall. The reason for this blow does not seem to be very clear, but Bell is believed to have said something to Dodworth, which resulted in his going away from the house. During the scuffle Bell lost his hat. Just at that moment the cry was raised 'Doddie is here,' this being the short name for Dodworth. Upon this Eaton ran up Young Street, where a fight took place between him and Dodworth. In the meantime the deceased also went up Young Street, in search of his hat, and it is stated that while he was there Eaton violently assaulted him, knocking him down two or three times.

Deceased was taken home seriously injured, and was attended to by Dr O'Meara, and subsequently Mr H. Lockwood, a house surgeon at the hospital. He was found to be suffering from concussion of the brain, and was, from the first, in a serious condition. He was kept in strict quiet, and carefully attended, but he succumbed to his injuries yesterday morning. The concussion of the brain would be caused either by a blow or a fall, and it is suggested by the friends of the prisoner that the deceased in the scuffle fell, and struck his head upon a stone. A post-mortem examination will probably take place, which may or may not throw some light upon this point. The circumstances are being carefully investigated by Detective Inspector Moody, and the case will be gone into on Monday next. The deceased man was 22 years of age, and he was a single man.

The scene of the fatal attack – Young Street in 2011

The case was heard within the month. In the *Leeds Mercury* of February 1, 1886 there was a report of the proceedings:

ALLEGED MANSLAUGHTER AT SHEFFIELD
James Eaton (17), hammer grinder, was charged with the manslaughter of Harvey Bell at Sheffield on the 2nd January last. Mr H. Cadman, who prosecuted, stated that on the night of the 2nd January prisoner and several other men were in the singing room of the Woodman Inn in Sheffield. During the evening prisoner acted as chairman over sort of a concert, and in the course of the proceedings he had a difference with some off those in the room. When the place was closed prisoner and deceased went out with others, and subsequently one of the company named Haigh struck deceased a light blow on the face. Prisoner then struck Bell with considerable violence and knocked him down. Bell's hat flew off and prisoner picked it up and ran away with it. Bell followed and, coming up with a man named Dodworth, had a quarrel with him and then again came into conflict with prisoner who, placing

Bell's hat on his head, struck him a heavy blow which caused him to fall to the ground, and to strike his head violently against a large wooden gate. Bell, in fact, was so severely treated that he shouted 'Murder', 'Watch', 'Police' and then said, 'Are you going to murder me or what do you want?' After that he was allowed to go, covered with blood. A friend met him and took him home. On the 5th January a medical man was called in, but shortly afterwards Bell died. It was then discovered that his death was caused by a fracture of the skull which led to compression of the brain. At an inquest on the deceased the jury returned a verdict of manslaughter against the prisoner. Mr C. Mellor, for the defence, contended that it could not be said with certainty who had struck the blow which caused Bell's death, for in the melee there must have been a good deal of confusion. The jury did not think that the evidence against the prisoner was strong enough to warrant them in saying that it was he who inflicted the fatal injury. He was therefore acquitted.

Given the facts it seemed the correct decision. No one could say with certainty that James Eaton struck the fatal blow, so there was only one possible verdict. However, there was no doubt that Eaton could consider himself fortunate to escape prison. The witnesses to the assault all said that it was Eaton who used considerable violence, striking Bell a heavy blow. The prosecution may have had more success in securing a conviction if they had brought a lesser charge of, say, actual bodily harm against Eaton.

This 1870 photograph of the Woodman Inn is taken from Peter Machan's book *Lost Sheffield – Portrait of a Victorian City*. If you were expecting a drab, grimy red-brick industrial pub, the type of which was commonplace in nineteenth-century Sheffield, you will be surprised to see that it was instead a rather delightful affair. Douglas Lamb's book *A Pub On Every Corner* places the Woodman Inn at just about where the big red-brick building (which is still known to many as the Manpower Services building, although it hasn't been called that for a long time) now is at the bottom of The Moor, on the right-hand side leaving town. It opened in 1833.

Napier Street – where Bell lived – photographed in 2011

CHAPTER 21

AN APPALLING DISASTER AT MATTHEW STREET, 1886

'They were frantic with grief with the possibility of their having been crushed'

APPALLING DISASTER to CHILDREN AT SHEFFIELD

Matthew Street is located in the Shalesmoor district of Sheffield, running off Doncaster Street and parallel to Hoyle Street. In the late nineteenth century the area was a hive of 'little mesters' workshops, small iron and steel works and typical late Victorian working-class housing. On August 25, 1886, at around five o'clock in the evening, eight children met their deaths here. The *News of the World* of August 29, 1886 gave details of what happened:

APPALLING DISASTER IN SHEFFIELD – EIGHT CHILDREN KILLED

On Wednesday evening a terrible accident occurred at the works of Messrs Daniel Doncaster and Sons, steel converters, in Sheffield. Their premises are situated in a densely populated part of the town and are skirted on the right by Matthew Street. On this was the warehouse where there were stored steel and iron bars roughly estimated at from 600 to 1,000 tons; the greater portion of this pile was stored against the wall which, in addition, supported the roofs. About 5 o'clock the wall suddenly gave way and fell into the street, carrying with it the immense mass of steel with the timbers of the roofs and slates. There was a report as of thunder but for several minutes nothing could be seen for the dense cloud of dust which rose high into the air. The people living at the opposite side of the street came to their doors in alarm and had their attention immediately attracted by the screams of two children who had been seated close to their doorsteps and who were nearly covered by debris. The children were liberated and found to be little injured.

In the road lay the steel piled up to a height of about 10 feet, and as several children had been seen a few minutes before playing under the warehouse wall the worst fears were entertained as to their fate. The workmen of Messrs Doncaster, of Messrs Southern and Richardson and neighbouring firms at once commenced to remove the steel but when it is stated that some of the bars were as much as three or four men could lift the nature of the task before them may be imagined. The chief constable, with a strong force of police, arrived and their services found to be very valuable in keeping back the crowd, for news of the disaster had quickly spread, and not only Matthew Street but all adjacent streets were blocked by the excited people. After some tons of metal had been removed it was decide to open passages into the mass, the more readily to ascertain whether any bodies were buried or not for the parents of five children had already reported them missing, and they were frantic with grief with the possibility of their having been crushed.

The men worked with energy, and by seven o'clock one opening in the metal had been made and underneath were found the remains of three children, mangled almost beyond recognition. A stretcher was brought and the bodies were removed to a room in the works. A little later another body was found and was identified from the clothing as that of a boy called Cullingworth, whose parents keep a tavern close by. The work of removing the metal now proceeded more rapidly and by nine o'clock three more bodies had been found, making seven in all. By this time the authorities had satisfied themselves that if there were more bodies under the metal, of which there was still an immense mass to remove, life must be extinct, and it was decided to suspend work until next morning.

The following is a list of the dead – Martha Armitage aged 10 years and John Armitage aged two, children of John Armitage, Hoyle Street; Henry Crisp aged six years, whose parents live in Adelphi Street; William Cullingworth, aged seven years, son of Tom Cullingworth of the Burnt Tree Tavern, Hoyle Street; Clifford Anderson aged seven years, whose parents live in Burnt Tree Lane; Samuel Oates, five-year-old son of John Oates, table blade grinder, Hoyle Street; William Henry Ward aged five, son of a table blade grinder.

During an examination of the bodies, some heartrending scenes were witnessed. Fathers and mothers came forward and identified their dead children by their garments, which alone afforded a means of identification. Two children were also removed to the infirmary suffering from severe injuries. The wall was 25 yards long and 18 feet in height. A person who was near the spot at the time of the accident said that two sharp reports like pistol shots were heard and then a great crash and clouds of dust obscured everything as the mingled bricks and mortar and metal fell in confused masses.

Thursday morning's search among the debris revealed another body, that of Herbert Crookes, aged five-and-a-half years old. His corpse was fearfully injured, and the father could only identify it by its clothing. On Friday, the Sheffield Coroner opened an inquest. The bodies were identified by the parents of the children and the Coroner, having granted certificates for burial, intimated his intention of having an inspection of the premises prior to taking further evidence, and adjourned the inquest for that purpose. Messrs Doncaster expressed their great grief at the occurrence and offered the Coroner every facility in the conduct of the inquiry.

William Cullingworth was buried in Sheffield's General Cemetery: Burial No. 14357 Grave No. U1-3. Henry Crisp was buried in Burngreave Cemetery: Grave No. V3-31

Matthew Street playground, around 1930 (courtesy Sheffield Local Studies Library)

Matthew Street in 2011. Doncaster's old cementation furnace can be seen in the background.

CHAPTER 22

THE TRAGIC DEATHS OF TWO WILLIAM CULLINGWORTHS

'The stands are too often so rickety and perilous'

William Cullingworth was one of the eight children killed in the Matthew Street wall collapse (see previous chapter). His father Tom was the landlord of the Burnt Tree Tavern, which stood at No.83 Hoyle Street, at its junction with Burnt Tree Lane. Matthew Street runs parallel to Hoyle Street and also has a junction with Burnt Tree Lane. All three roads still exist, but their layout is much changed.

Young William was buried at Sheffield General Cemetery, which lies between Cemetery Road and Stalker Lees Road. His grave reference is: Burial No. 14357, Grave No. U13, buried August 29, 1886. The cemetery records also show that another William Cullingworth is buried there. His grave reference is: Burial No. 3986, Grave No. G49, buried May 20, 1874. This William was 43 years old, and a victualler by trade, who resided at the New Turk's Head public house, No.118 Scotland Street.

One of the organisers of tours of the General Cemetery has confirmed that the two Williams were related (uncle and nephew?), and that the older one also died as a result of a tragic accident when he and his friends went for a day at the races. The *Sheffield Daily Telegraph* of March 25, 1874 explained what occurred:

FALL OF A STAND AT LINCOLN RACES
SEVERAL SHEFFIELD MEN INJURED
We learn by telegraph that while the Carholme Stakes were being run at the Lincoln Race Meeting, yesterday afternoon, one of the temporary stands fell, carrying with it a crowd of people, many of whom were injured. Amongst the persons who received the most serious wounds was Mr William Cullingworth, landlord of the New Turk's Head, Scotland Street. Several other Sheffield men who were present also received cuts and bruises, and were removed to the Hospital, where Mr Cullingworth lies in a most critical state, his spine having been dreadfully injured.

Freeman's Journal of the same day also covered the accident but added far more background detail and comment:

The melancholy accident which occurred yesterday at Lincoln Races, where a number of people were more or less injured by the fall of one of the stands, is one more proof of the unaccountable recklessness or rather negligence so frequently displayed in the building of these temporary edifices. Hardly a racing season passes that is not unpleasantly marked by casualties of this kind. Even on race courses, otherwise creditably managed, the stands are too often so rickety and perilous that the wonder is how the catalogue of disaster is not vastly more inclusive. As a matter of fact it is only when these dangerous man-traps kill or maim their dozens or their scores that any noise is made about a state of things which calls imperatively for stern interference. The fall of a stand is so common that it is not noticed unless life or limb suffer thereby. There ought to be little difficulty in securing safety and stability in these necessary structures. That the architect, the contractor, or the proprietor is liable for consequences is very poor satisfaction to those who suffer by his carelessness, his hurry, or his greed. It is certain, also, that the constant repetition of accidents arising wholly from these causes must tend to scare the public, and in this way bring a punishment which might be certainly escaped by providing such accommodation as could be availed of with confidence. We have seen grand stands ornamentally or even elegantly built, which it was, however, impossible to use with comfort, for the simple reason that strength formed no feature of the building, which swayed and shook with every movement of its occupants. So long as those having the management of race meetings do not take this important matter energetically into their own hands, so long we shall have to regret such lamentable occurrences as that which has converted the Lincoln Races from a place of carnival to an arena of mourning. This evil can certainly be cured by the plain system of a proper supervision and sufficient inspection. A miserable feature of the present deplorable accident was the inhuman treatment of a poor man who had both his legs smashed by the falling timbers of the stand. While he lay on the ground in dire agonies, and unable to protect himself, some wretches actually picked his pockets.

A day later the *Leeds Mercury* gave a report and referred to the fact that William Cullingworth was at first feared dead:

THE STAND ACCIDENT AT LINCOLN RACES
A serious accident occurred at the race course at Lincoln on Tuesday. About three o'clock, when the race for the Carholme Stakes was being run, a temporary stand, erected by the race committee inside the betting enclosure, collapsed, burying a number of its occupants among the wreck. Nearly sixty people were injured. The more serious cases were taken to the hospital, others were taken to the railway station and sent home. One poor fellow from Sheffield was carried to the hospital as dead, but it was found that, though his case was a very serious one, he still breathed. A pickpocket was caught in the act of easing one of the injured of his watch as he lay on the ground senseless, and was at once taken into custody.

William's injuries were to his spine and his thigh. His was a very serious case. There was one other injured man from Sheffield; W. H. Pearson, a fish salesman, who had contusions to his ankle and knee. Other injured parties came from Doncaster, London, Croydon, Nottingham, Retford, Wakefield and Hull. A fifteen-year-old girl from Leeds suffered a spine injury. Despite the disaster, the race meeting continued, but the next race, the Brocklesby Stakes, started 25 minutes late.

William never recovered. The accident happened on March 24, 1874 but he did not die until May 16, a period in excess of seven weeks, during which time he must have experienced indescribable pain as a result of his injuries. The death certificate indicates that William died in Lincoln, so his return to Sheffield was in a coffin.

CHAPTER 23

THE SHOCKING DEATH OF ARTHUR COLEMAN, FIRVALE WORKHOUSE, 1886

'In a destitute state, stark naked, and totally alone in a dark room, they were then, for the second time, taken to the workhouse'

Arthur Coleman died, aged eleven, in 1886. The Census of five years earlier shows him living at No.49 Pea Croft, Sheffield, with his father Michael, mother Bridget and brothers Michael and Frederick. Pea Croft was located in the area extending east from Solly Street, towards the junction of Tenter Street and West Bar. What used to be Pea Croft is now part of Solly Street. The whole Crofts area of Sheffield in the mid-to-late nineteenth century was a grim district of cramped terraced dwellings housing the poorest quarter of society. The photographs (courtesy Sheffield Local Studies Library) show Pea Croft in around 1900. Between the Census and the events related here, records show that the family had moved first to Hawley Croft and then to Water Lane, which ran between, and parallel to, Snig Hill and Waingate.

A report in the *Illustrated Police News* on September 18, 1886 gave details of the inquest into young Arthur's death:

An inquest was opened on Saturday at Sheffield on the body of Arthur Coleman, aged eleven years, son of Michael Coleman, a hawker. The boy was seen to drop in the street from exhaustion, and he and an elder brother were taken to the workhouse. They were found to be in a most emaciated and starved state. Arthur died on Wednesday and when he was weighed he was only 2st 4lb 10oz. The average weight of a boy that age is 6 stone. The father said when he left home in the mornings he had always given the mother 4d or 6d to buy food for the day, and he now believed she had spent the money on drink. The inquiry was adjourned for the attendance of the mother, who is ill, the Coroner remarking that in all probability one or both parents would be committed for manslaughter.

A further report appeared in the *Sheffield and Rotherham Independent* on September 30, 1886:

THE ALLEGED DEATH FROM STARVATION IN SHEFFIELD.

WARRANTS FOR MANSLAUGHTER GRANTED.

At the Sheffield Town Hall, yesterday, before Mr Skelton Cole, Mr F. Neal, solicitor, applied, on behalf the London Society for the Prevention of Cruelty to Children, for a warrant on a charge of manslaughter against the parents of a child named Arthur Coleman, aged eleven years, who died in the Fir Vale Workhouse on the 8th instant. In making the application, Mr Neal stated that he had been instructed on behalf of the London Society for the Prevention of Cruelty to Children to make an application for a warrant against Michael Coleman and Bridget Coleman, the parents of the child. He explained that the allegation of the prosecution was that by systematic neglect and cruelty its death was hastened, or, in other words, that the child's death took place sooner than under natural causes it would have done. He went on to state that the usual inquest was held, and that two medical men swore that death had been accelerated by neglect and cruelty. Upon that the Coroner intimated that the jury would not be justified in finding a verdict of manslaughter, whereupon they found that the child died from a disease of the lungs, but that this was probably accelerated by the neglect and cruelty of the parents. The society which he represented now wished to have that ruling of the Coroner brought before the Court, so that it might ultimately be taken to the Assizes and the decision of the judges obtained on the point.

Replying to Mr Cole, Mr Neal further stated that repeated cautions had been given to the parents of the child as to their treatment of it and other members of the family. For the past two years the child had been suffering for want of food, and on one occasion the children were found in the house entirely naked. The Bench granted the warrant asked for.

The following day the same paper carried another report of the case:

THE ALLEGED STARVATION CASE
MAGISTERIAL PROCEEDINGS
At the Town Hall yesterday, before Mr S. Roberts, Jun., and Mr John Wilson, Michael Coleman and Bridget Coleman were brought up in custody on a charge of manslaughter. The circumstances, which were investigated before the Coroner's jury, were such as to reveal a deplorable amount of neglect and cruelty on the part of the deceased's parents, and the jury, although stopping short of a verdict of manslaughter, expressed their feeling that the parents were morally guilty of the child's death.

Mr Arthur Neal prosecuted and stated that the circumstances under which the prosecution was preferred were these. On the 4th Sept., in the evening, a man named James Cooper was near the New Market, when he saw the deceased child in the centre of a crowd, utterly exhausted and unable to walk. He carried the child to his home in Water Lane, and communicated with the police. Police Constable Porter, considering it a proper case for the parish authorities, informed Mr

Davenport, the relieving officer, who gave an order for the attendance of Mr Harrison, the medical officer, by whose recommendation the whole family was removed to the workhouse, where the child died. At the inquest two medical officers swore that in their opinion death was caused by congestion of the lungs, accelerated by starvation, privation and neglect. The inquest was adjourned, and in the interval the society Mr Neal represented became acquainted with the case and instituted enquiries. At the adjourned inquest evidence was produced that as long ago as 1884, Mr Barber, the relieving officer, found the deceased and other children of the accused in a state of very great neglect; that in September 1885, he again visited the house and found the children in a state of nudity in the middle of the day, and bearing evident marks of privation and neglect. The evidence of neighbours in Water Lane also showed that when the child had asked for food it had met with blows; that it had been systematically neglected, and that it had constantly suffered from lack of food; that it had been taken out at 9.30 in the morning begging; kept out all the day, and brought home late in the evening without any regular food; and that the child grew thinner and thinner, and weaker and weaker.

On the 28th of August a direct act of cruelty was witnessed. The female prisoner took the child into the yard, stripped it, and put it into a tub of water as deep as to its chest. She left it in the water for upwards of an hour; it was crying and complaining the whole time, and its cries were met with blows to the head with a key until blood flowed. This would be testified by a man named Wright, who would also say that on the very morning of the day when the child was carried home from the New Market, he told the female prisoner that the child was not able to go out, and in almost pathetic language pleaded with the prisoner that the child was dying, but the mother insisted on its going out. Six or seven persons would give evidence of a similar nature – that the conduct of the female prisoner towards the child had been cruel and unnatural.

The post-mortem examination revealed tubercular disease sufficient to account for death, and that there was an entire absence of fat, and other signs pointing to privation, starvation and neglect. If, by neglect, the child's death had been accelerated, then there was a common law liability on the part of the parents to provide food and necessaries, and a statutory liability to provide medical aid. What he had said already applied more particularly to the mother. The father stated that he had been accustomed to give his wife 6d a day to provide for the child, and he made no allegation of actual cruelty against him, or that he was guilty of wilful neglect or wasting his time and money in drink, but what the prosecution said concerning him was that he must have known how the child was being neglected and that his wife was squandering the money he gave her on drink; and if he was so wickedly careless what became of his children as to continue to trust to that source of supply for their necessities he was neglecting his duty as a parent, and was equally guilty with his wife.

Sarah Mosey, domestic servant at the Old House at Home, Water Lane, said that the prisoners had lived in that house, and she had heard the female prisoner tell the child when he asked for bread that he must wait till he got some. She (witness) and other people had given the child food. Having lived in the same room as them, she had seen the father give the child food, but never once the mother. The female prisoner used to get drunk every day.

The Chairman asked Mr Neal whether he could refer the Bench to any other case in which a conviction for manslaughter had been obtained upon simple evidence of the neglect of the parents in not sending the children to the workhouse when they had not food to give to them. Mr Neal said he had not been able to find such a case, but the way he put the case was this: that the prisoners were bound by statute law to find the child with food and medical aid, that they knew it required both, that they carelessly neglected to find it either; and that this accelerated death. That was what he complained of – that they were doing an unlawful act in neglecting to find the child food and medical aid, and in consequence of that unlawful act the death was accelerated.

Mr John Wilson: 'Supposing that they were unable to find the food?'

Mr Neal said they were bound by common law to find food if they were able, and by statute law even if they were unable, for the statute made no mention of ability. The depositions were then read over, and the prisoners were committed for trial, the Chairman saying, 'We think there is evidence of neglect and cruelty, and it will be for the jury to say whether they will convict.'

The next report is from the *Leeds Mercury*, November 20, 1886. Arthur's parents appeared before Mr Justice Hawkins at the Yorkshire Winter Assizes held in York, charged with the manslaughter of their son:

AN UNSUSTAINED CHARGE OF MANSLAUGHTER
Michael Coleman (37), hawker, and his wife Bridget Coleman (35), hawker, were indicted for the manslaughter of Arthur Coleman, at

Sheffield on the 8th September last. Mr Kershaw and Mr Waugh prosecuted at the instance of the London Society for the Prevention of Cruelty to Children. The prisoners were undefended.

The prisoners were in a very humble station in life, the father being a hawker of paraffin while the mother begged in the streets. They had two children living with them and for the last five years when the relieving officer called he always found them in a neglected and half starved condition. On one occasion in 1885 when the officer called he found the children in a destitute state, stark naked, and totally alone in a dark room, and they were then for the second time taken to the workhouse. The child who had died seemed to been systematically neglected. After hearing the medical evidence his Lordship observed that there was no one who sympathised with poor children more than he did, no one who felt more indignation against parents who neglected their children and caused them suffering and privation and no one who felt more strongly that such misconduct should receive the punishment that was its due. But he also had to bear in mind that justice demanded that no man be convicted of a serious offence unless the evidence against him was thoroughly established. Mr Kershaw may have sustained a prosecution against the prisoners under the statute for not giving the child proper food and nourishment but in the present case he would himself see this difficulty. Mr Kershaw stated that he would not proceed with the evidence and the jury formally returned a verdict of not guilty. His Lordship, in discharging the prisoners, stated that he did not wish it to be understood that in that particular case for very special reasons, the charge of manslaughter could not be sustained, the law should not punish with very great severity all parents and others who ill use children in their care.

The ruling may be difficult to understand, but the problem was that the prosecution charged the Colemans with manslaughter, when the more appropriate charge given the facts of the case would have been neglect and cruelty. The surgeon was unequivocal in his statement that the immediate cause of death was tubercular disease and that in his opinion there was no doubt that this was accelerated by privation and exposure and want of food, but no one could state for definite that the neglect and starvation accelerated Arthur's death. Of course, exposure, privation, and want of food were endemic amongst the working classes in late Victorian England. If every case was prosecuted, the whole criminal justice system would have collapsed.

Arthur was laid to rest in Sheffield's Roman Catholic Cemetery in the beautiful Rivelin Valley, a marked contrast to the squalor and misery he had endured during his brief life in Sheffield. His grave reference is: Grave Number 12, Section JA of St Michael's RC Cemetery, Rivelin. His mother outlived him by just a few months, being buried in the same cemetery on February 4, 1887, grave reference: Grave Number 6, Section NA of St Michael's RC Cemetery, Rivelin. She was not buried alongside her son.

With cruel irony, 121 years later, in the autumn of 2007, barely a mile from where Arthur Coleman once lived with his parents, a three-year-old girl died of cruelty and neglect. This time the mother was charged with manslaughter and received a twelve-year prison sentence for the pain and suffering she inflicted on her daughter.

CHAPTER 24

DOUBLE DEATH ON WEST STREET, 1886

'His visits were indeed more frequent than could be desired by Mr and Mrs Jubb'

In the burial registers of Sheffield's City Road Cemetery there appears the following entry:

Jubb, Margaret (Married (shot), age 31). Died at Royal Hotel, West Street; Buried on December 4, 1886 in Consecrated Ground; Grave Number 11805, Section W of City Road Cemetery, Sheffield.

It certainly is not often that a burial record includes the phrase 'married (shot)'! So what were the circumstances of Margaret Jubb's death? The *Manchester Guardian* of December 2, 1886 explained how the affair unfurled:

SHOCKING MURDER AND SUICIDE IN SHEFFIELD
About noon yesterday, a terrible murder was committed in Sheffield followed by the suicide of the murderer, a German named Usnich, who shot Mrs Jubb, the landlady of a small public house called the Royal Hotel, West Street. Mrs Jubb and her husband had only occupied the Royal Hotel for about three months. The husband, John Jubb, was a table knife cutler in the employ of Messrs Rodgers and Sons: the house therefore was principally left to the management of Mrs Jubb. Amongst other habitual frequenters of the house was a man named Joseph

*Usnich, a German employed as an engineer, who used to lodge with the
Jubbs when they occupied a private house in St Mary's Road. He had
recently lodged in Fitzwilliam Street, which is no great distance from
the Royal Hotel, and his visits were indeed more frequent than could be
desired by Mr and Mrs Jubb. Yesterday morning he was lounging
around the house apparently for several hours. He was there as early
as eight o'clock and spoke to the servant girl who was cleaning the
taproom. A short time before the murder he borrowed a newspaper and
went and sat at the bar apparently to read. Mrs Jubb was with the
servant girl, Mary Ellen Whittaker, and three of her four young
children in the kitchen, which is connected to the bar by a short
passage, when a rap was heard in the bar. Usnich had been sitting in
the bar a few minutes before Mrs Jubb went from the kitchen to meet
the call. She had not been there more than a minute when shots were
heard and the poor woman staggered along the passage to the kitchen,
calling to the servant girl that she was shot. She managed to reach the
kitchen but fell unconscious on the hearth. The shots reached the ears
of the neighbours and a number of people entered the hotel. A Mr
Freeman found what had occurred and the bar being empty imagined
that the murderer had escaped by the front door. It did not appear
however that anyone had come out of the house and Mr Freeman
obtained the assistance of the police. Police Constable Candling was
promptly in attendance and soon found the missing man, who was lying
dead behind the entrance door from the house into the bar. He had
apparently shot himself immediately after inflicting wounds upon Mrs
Jubb and had fallen against the door. Mrs Jubb, who had apparently
but one wound to the left breast, was removed to the hospital but
despite every attention the poor woman died about a quarter past one
o'clock, a little more than an hour after she was shot. The six-
chambered revolver with which the murder was committed was taken
possession of by Police Constable Candling. The body of the murderer
was afterwards moved to the mortuary. It had wounds to the breast and
the mouth, leading to the conclusion that he fired two shots at himself.*

*Prior to moving into the hotel the Jubbs lived at 168 St Mary's Road.
They were there about three years and during a large part of the time
Mr Jubb was ill and altogether unable to follow his employment. Mrs
Jubb, however, took in lodgers, mainly members of the theatrical
profession, and in other ways assisted to maintain the family. She is
spoken of as being a most industrious woman who worked hard to keep
her house clean, with her children respectable. Usnich went to lodge*

with them and whether there were grounds for suspicion or not there seems to be little doubt that Jubb became jealous of his wife. This was generally manifested when Jubb had some drink and on such occasions he and Usnich usually quarrelled. It does not seem clear that Mrs Jubb gave Usnich any encouragement or her husband ground for suspecting them.

The *Birmingham Daily Post* of December 4, 1886 reported on the subsequent inquest, in which it was learned that the killer's name was actually Husnik, and that he was Austrian, not German:

THE SHEFFIELD TRAGEDY
The coroner's enquiry regarding the murder of Margaret Jubb, wife of a Sheffield hotel-keeper, and the suicide of Joseph Husnik, the murderer, was held last evening at the Sheffield public hospital. Husnik, who was an Austrian, lodged with the Jubbs. A verdict of 'wilful murder' was returned in the case of the woman, and 'suicide' as regards Husnik.

The same day the *Manchester Guardian* also reported on the Coroner's enquiry and gave some additional information on the tragedy:

THE MURDER AND SUICIDE AT SHEFFIELD.

An inquest was held last evening on the body of Margaret Jubb, landlady of the Royal Hotel, West-street, Sheffield, who was murdered on Wednesday by an Austrian named Joseph Husnik.

An inquiry took place at the same time with regard to the death of Husnik, who committed suicide by shooting himself immediately after the murder of Mrs Jubb. In Husnik's pockets two letters were found, both bewailing the conduct of Mrs Jubb, who, according to Husnik, had sworn him eternal love, and had broken her pledges after obtaining money from him. One of the letters was in these words: 'My dearest darling love, You are wishing seperreshen from you loving hart. To oblige you I will bury my true heart and sepperreyt as soon as possible, so that I be unable to love you agen becos you now that a man without hart cannot love. Your obliging J. H.'

It was proved that Husnik had deliberately prepared for the committal of the crime. He fired in all five shots, three of which were directed against himself. The jury found that Husnik wilfully murdered Mrs Jubb and committed suicide himself, but that as to the state of his mind there was no evidence.

From the reports it is difficult to come to a definitive conclusion, but a possible explanation is that Mrs Jubb did borrow money from Husnik (perhaps to fund the move to the Royal Hotel), a transaction that Husnik misread. Clearly Mr Jubb had his suspicions about Husnik and his wife, but that was all they were. Mrs Jubb may have then reneged on her promises to pay back Husnik, which led him to kill her.

Joseph Husnik's funeral was reported in the *Sheffield and Rotherham Independent* on December 8, 1886. It mentions that the funeral took place the previous evening; it sounds positively 'gothic' as it would have been dark when the hearse left the workhouse and arrived at the cemetery:

THE WEST STREET TRAGEDY
The final scene in the West Street tragedy was enacted last evening, when the body of Joseph Husnik was interred in the cemetery at Intake. As the deceased had no relatives or friends in this country, the burial was undertaken by the Workhouse authorities. About five o'clock the hearse was driven to the hospital, in the charge of two paupers. The body was then placed in a Workhouse coffin, and the hearse proceeded to Intake. No funeral service was read either in the chapel or at the graveside. As it was not known when the funeral would take place, there were no spectators. Mr H. P. Collinson, clerk to the Burial Board, made the necessary arrangements for the funeral and was in attendance at the interment. Notwithstanding that Mrs Oates, the deceased's landlady, has made every effort to find some means of communication with his relatives, she has so far been unsuccessful, but she entertains a hope that some clue may be afforded by some people with whom he once lived at Derby.

City Road Cemetery's burial records have the following entry:

Husnik, Joseph (Engineer, age 27); Died at Royal Hotel, West Street; Buried on December 7, 1886 in Unconsecrated Ground; Grave Number 12968, Section BB of City Road Cemetery, Sheffield.

Both victim and killer were buried at City Road Cemetery, but Margaret in consecrated ground and Husnik in unconsecrated ground. As a footnote, Margaret's husband John Jubb did not live long after the tragedy. He is buried with his wife in the same grave:

Jubb, John (Table Knife Hafter, age 42); Died at Firvale Workhouse; Buried on June 23, 1892 in Consecrated Ground; Grave Number 11805, Section W of City Road Cemetery, Sheffield.

His death in the workhouse seems to indicate that his illness deteriorated after his wife's death. But what happened to their four children?

The site of the former Royal Hotel on West Street

Douglas Lamb's book *A Pub On Every Corner* informs that the Royal Hotel stood at No.86 West Street, opposite the end of Carver Street, and a few doors down from the original Saddle public house. The Royal opened in 1833 and closed down in 1893, coincidentally or not, soon after John Jubb's death.

There is one final unusual twist to this episode; there was an entry in the *Manchester Guardian* of July 6, 1885 showing that J. Husnik and H. Merryman of Sheffield had applied for a patent for a self-feeding penholder – from innovative engineer to lovelorn murderer in under two years. Whether the patent was granted is not known.

CHAPTER 25

A VIOLENT ATTACK ON A GIRL, SHALESMOOR, 1888

'He seized her by both shoulders, planted his knee in her back, and pulled her over, kicking her as she fell'

The *Sheffield and Rotherham Independent* of September 25, 1888 referred to an assault in Club Mill Yard, resulting in the death of a young Sheffield woman named Rebecca Evans, who, it was reported, suffered a broken neck. The attack had occurred the previous evening:

MURDEROUS ASSAULT IN CLUB MILL YARD.

A GIRL'S NECK BROKEN.

Quite an epidemic of shockingly sensational incidents has broken out in Sheffield. The last to be added to the list occurred yesterday evening, and created the greatest possible excitement in the neighbourhood where the principal parties to it reside—not it must be admitted one of the most savoury localities in the town.

For some time past there has lived with her father and sisters – her mother being dead – at 29, Smithfield, a young woman named Rebecca

Evans, aged 17. She was employed in the table-knife trade, and worked at Messrs Norton's, in Cambridge Street. Soon after six o'clock in the evening she was standing at the end of Blue Boy Street with two companions, named Mary Pigott and Sarah Nuttall. When asked to walk down Allen Street with them she replied that she dared not go, as there was a young fellow who 'owed her a grudge'. She alluded to a youth, aged 15, named Frederick Lait, a grinder, who lived with his parents at 41, Trinity Street. The girl Evans and Lait had known each other many years, had played together as children, and they had seen each other earlier in the evening. He had then made provoking remarks to the girl, and she had retaliated by calling him names, and as a parting shot had told him 'to go and get a clean shirt on'. The insinuation that his linen was not as clean as it should be seems to have exasperated him, and, knowing that, she was afraid to go down the street where he was likely to be. In a few minutes Lait, who was with John Lomas and two other youths, came up the street. On seeing them Evans ran up Club Mill Yard, and Lait followed her. He caught her, and pushed her with great violence against a bakehouse door. She endeavoured to escape from him again, when he seized her by both shoulders, planted his knee in her back, and pulled her over, kicking her as she fell. He then ran away.

A table knife cutler named Philip Carr, who lives in Craven Street, was in the Club Mill Yard at the time, and seeing the girl fall he went to her. He ran down the yard, and seeing some girls about asked if any of them knew her. Two of them went to Evans and then asked Carr if he would hold her while they went for her sister. He did so, and in a minute or two Sarah Ann Evans came, and the girl was carried to her home in Smithfield, which is close by. Mr F. Kitson, landlord of the Eagle and Child public house, in Smithfield, hearing that the girl was injured, ran for a doctor. He went to Mr Reckless's surgery and there promptly obtained medical aid. In the meantime the sister had called in Mrs Mary Ann Holt, who lives at 27, Smithfield, and on her reaching the house she found that the girl was dead. There was no doubt that her neck was broken. The sister, Sarah Ann Evans, saw Lait a few minutes after and she told him 'He would catch it'. He asked, 'What have I done?' She answered, 'You have killed her.' He said, 'I don't care.'

Information of what had occurred soon reached Police Constable Scott, who was in the neighbourhood, and, having satisfied himself of the death of the girl, he went in search of Lait. He found him in Allen Street, and took him to the Police Office. In answer to the charge of having caused the death of the girl Evans, he denied that he had done anything to her. About ten o'clock the body of the girl was taken to the mortuary, there to await the inquest.

One of the most important witnesses who will be called will be the lad John Lomas, who works at the Hallamshire Steel and File Works. He was with Lait and saw him run Evans up the street, and when she reached the bakehouse door he pushed her violently, and she fell with either her head or arm against it. She commenced to run again, and on his overtaking her, Lait seized her by both shoulders, pulled her back, and kicked her on the shoulders as she was falling. He ran away, and on coming up with his companions, he said, he said, 'Come on lads; let us be off now,' and he hurried up Allen Street. The girls Pigott and Nuttall may also be examined, for they were last in conversation with Evans, and heard her express her dread of meeting Lait. Her sister, Sarah Ann Evans, was present when the two met earlier in the day, and she knows what passed between them. Mr Carr saw the girl fall, but he did not see Lait with her. He thinks the girl ran a few yards after Lait hit her, and then fell backwards. He was at her side directly, but she never spoke – only gave one or two gasps and died.

Lait was apprehended and the following day was brought before the local magistrate on the charge of manslaughter, but the hearing was adjourned pending the Coroner's inquest, and somewhat surprisingly Lait was released on bail. It is also surprising that Lait was charged only with manslaughter; unlawful killings without malice or intent are considered as manslaughter but if the newspaper report is accurate, Lait's attack on Rebecca seemed to show both malice and intent, and perhaps warranted a murder charge.

PRISONER BEFORE THE STIPENDIARY
At the Sheffield Town Hall, yesterday, before the Stipendiary, Frederick Lait, aged 15, described as a grinder, living with his parents at 41, Trinity Street, was charged with the manslaughter of Rebecca Evans, 17 years of age, in Club Mill Yard, on Monday evening. The prisoner is a diminutive, respectable-looking lad, and his apparently unconcerned bearing as he stood in the defendant's box seemed to indicate that he was far from realising the seriousness of his position. The proceedings were very brief, lasting only a few minutes. As soon as the case was called on Detective Inspector Smith applied for a remand until Thursday, to allow the Coroner's inquest on the body of the deceased girl being first held. This was granted by the Stipendiary, and the boy's father then applied for bail. No opposition was made to this course, and

the prisoner was accordingly liberated, his father and one surety being bound in the sum of £10 each to bring him up on Thursday next.

The 'I don't care' indifference Lait showed at the time of the crime also manifested itself before the magistrate, when he appeared to be unconcerned at the seriousness of the offence. The events of the Coroner's inquest, reported in the *Sheffield and Rotherham Independent,* are therefore perplexing:

THE SAD DEATH OF A GIRL IN SHEFFIELD

The adjourned inquiry into the death of Rebecca Evans, 17 years of age, the girl who it had been alleged was killed by a lad named Frederick Lait, was held at the Mortuary, yesterday afternoon, before the Deputy Coroner, Mr B. Bagshawe. Mr Fairburn attended on behalf of Lait, who was also present. The theory that the girl died through having her neck broken by a kick was shown by the gentlemen who made the post-mortem examination to be a groundless one. The cause of death was of a natural kind – a fit induced by excitement shortly after a meal – and, although as Mr Bagshawe told Lait, he had committed a most brutal attack on her, he had committed no legal offence. He was, therefore, discharged by Mr Bagshawe with a severe reprimand. The verdict of the jury was in accordance with the medical evidence.

Mr Charles Atkin, surgeon, was the first witness called, and he stated that he made a post-mortem examination of the deceased last Friday. Externally there were no marks of violence, nor were there any internally. There was no dislocation or fracture, or any effusion of any kind. The head and brain were in a good normal condition. He found evidence of disease in the left lung; the lungs, stomach, and liver were all congested. The stomach was full of semi-digested food.

The Deputy Coroner: 'Did you observe anything else whatever which excited suspicion or would tend to indicate the cause of death?

Witness: 'None whatever.'

'Assuming the deceased had been unusually excited after having just had a full meal, might that induce a fit?'

'It might in a person so predisposed.'

'Was she predisposed to a fit?'

'It is impossible to say.'

141

'Assuming a person was so predisposed, would the excitement be likely to bring on a fit?'

'Yes.'

A Juror: 'What was the cause of the discolouration at the back of the neck?'

Witness: 'That was post-mortem.'

Another Juror: 'And the head rolled about?'

Witness: 'I must say that when Mr Reckless and I examined her shortly after death, and till we had examined the spinal cord, we thought that the neck was broken. The reason the head moved about so easily was that the muscles of the neck were very slim. But with all dead people the head will move from side to side.'

Mr Fairburn: 'What, in your opinion, was the cause of death?'

Witness: 'My opinion is that she died from natural causes, and that the natural causes was a fit.'

A Juror: 'Accelerated by excitement?'

Witness: 'Possibly.'

Mr Fairburn: 'Violence had nothing to do with it?'

Witness: 'There were no marks of violence on the body.'

In reply to the Deputy Coroner, he said there could not be the slightest doubt that the spinal column was uninjured. The post-mortem examination was made in the presence of Mr Reckless and two unqualified medical gentlemen.

Mary Pigott, who lived in a court off Edward Street, stated she heard Lait threaten Rebecca Evans, then saw him chase her up Smithfield, and strike her once. Lomas, of No.9 Cotton Mill Walk, said that he witnessed the whole of Lait's attack on Rebecca and described it in detail. George Widdison, a milk carrier, of No.47 Allen Street, stated that he saw Lait run after the deceased along Smithfield, then, at the entry to Club Mill Yard, he kicked her in the back, and left the scene. Philip Carr, of No.12 Craven Street, a table-knife cutler, was outside the Club Mill public house and saw the deceased run by and then fall. He went to fetch Mary Pigott, who recognised the girl as Rebecca Evans. When he went to Evans, she was still alive. Sarah Ann Evans, sister of Rebecca, deposed that she had never seen her sister or any of the family have a fit.

The *Sheffield and Rotherham Independent* report continued:

> *The Deputy Coroner said that all further evidence would simply confirm the statements of the witnesses who saw the occurrence, and as the facts seemed to have been pretty clearly brought out by the witnesses examined, it was unnecessary to call any more. He then summed up, and told the jury that in his opinion there was nothing to warrant a verdict of manslaughter, whatever they might think of the conduct of Lait. The jury returned a verdict 'that the deceased died from natural causes immediately after an attack made upon her by Frederick Lait'. The Deputy Coroner, addressing Lait, said he had had an extremely narrow escape of being committed for manslaughter. He had made a most brutal attack upon the deceased, and apparently intended more violence than was actually found to have been committed when the deceased's body was examined. He must consider himself extremely lucky to get off on that occasion. If he did a similar thing again he would probably be committed for manslaughter, and then he would have an opportunity of thinking over the result of such acts. He deserved a good horse-whipping for what he did to the deceased. He appeared to be one of those boys who wanted correcting, and correcting frequently. The lad then left, accompanied by his father.*

The surgeon had asserted that violence had played no part in Rebecca's death, and that there were no marks either internally or externally to indicate a violent struggle. The discolouration at the back of the neck was, he said, produced post-mortem, and was due entirely to her head 'wagging' about after she had died. This version is particularly difficult to believe. The consistent descriptions of the assault given by several witnesses indicate that this was a vicious assault. Even the Deputy Coroner remarked in his summing up that Lait had made a 'brutal attack' on Rebecca; Mr Atkin did not adequately explain how he could be so certain that the discolouration at the back of the neck was post mortem, and nobody pressed him on this point. If it was post mortem, it must have happened within minutes of her death. However, Mr Atkin's deposition was sufficient to satisfy the Deputy Coroner and the jury. Perhaps by now Lait was in full realisation of his possible fate, but it must not be forgotten that he was a boy appearing on a serious charge in an adult court. For this, at least, he deserved a little sympathy.

However, it could easily be argued that had Lait not attacked Rebecca she would have lived. Her sister reported at the inquest that neither Rebecca nor her relatives had ever been subject to fits, and the surgeon remarked that her brain, head and spinal cord were in 'good normal condition'. The Deputy

Coroner also contradicted himself when on the one hand he stated that there was 'nothing to warrant a charge of manslaughter' and then proceeded to tell Lait that he had an 'extremely narrow escape from being committed for manslaughter'. On the evidence presented at the inquest Lait should have been formally committed to trial for manslaughter and not merely released with a severe reprimand. And the irony is that had Rebecca lived, Lait would almost certainly have been found guilty of common assault, perhaps serving a prison term, but because she died he got away scot free. He was indeed an 'extremely lucky' boy. One wonders if he learned from his escape, and thereafter led a quiet and crime-free life.

Possibly he did, for there is no evidence of his having spent time in prison in later life. This was despite coming from a nomadic family, the head of which had a history of crime. The 1881 Census lists his father, also Frederick (aged 36 in 1881), as being born in Eye, Suffolk, and his mother, Hannah, as being born in Louth, Lincolnshire. Frederick junior was also born in Louth, but one brother, Walter (aged four in 1881), was born in Sheffield and another, Earnest (aged one in 1881), was born in Liverpool. At the time of the Census the family lived at No.147 Dunlop Street, Attercliffe. Frederick senior's occupation was as a coach painter; perhaps it was this line of work that took him from Suffolk to Lincolnshire, to Sheffield, to Liverpool and back to Sheffield, this time settling in the Shalesmoor area.

It was whilst in Louth that Frederick senior came to the attention of the courts. In June 1865 it was reported in the *Hull Packet and East Riding Times* that Lait (who also used the alias Smith) was charged with stealing a silver medal, eye-glasses, a medical instrument and clothing belonging to an elderly woman, Mary Pexton, with whom he lodged. Lait was convicted at Hull of a felony and sentenced to seven years' penal servitude, serving his time at the Portland Establishments for Male Convicts in Dorset, where the 1871 Census, which was taken in April of that year, recorded his presence. He was released after six years but was not long free of incarceration before he was in trouble again, this time with an accomplice, a woman named Ann Bateson. The *Police Gazette* of September 15, 1871 reported that the couple, travelling as man and wife, were being sought in connection with the stealing of a silver watch from a house in Louth. It is unlikely that Lait was apprehended for this offence because less than two years later he was married to Hannah, who gave birth to his son Frederick.

By 1901 the Lait family had moved from Sheffield to No.35 Scarsdale Road, Dronfield, north Derbyshire. Frederick junior, now a 28-year-old coal hewer, was still living at home, though he was now married, to Florence, and had children of his own, Bertha, aged seven, and Albert, aged six. However, the 1911 Census throws the family status into confusion. They are still at the same house in Dronfield, but Frederick senior and Hannah are no longer there, perhaps now dead. Bertha is now listed as Frederick junior's sister, not daughter, and there is also a nephew, four-year-old Samuel Siddall. This Census states that Frederick and Florence have been married for fourteen years but have no children. Albert Lait, now sixteen, is lodging at a house at Thorpe Hesley, Rotherham.

Smithfield in 2012. No.29, where Rebecca Evans lived, was on the right-hand side; Club Mill Yard, at No.20, was on the left.

All the streets mentioned in the newspaper reports still exist (even the intriguingly named Blue Boy Street), much changed, though Club Mill Yard, which stood at No.20 Smithfield, has been demolished. However, Smithfield is still there, running off Snow Lane (which itself runs off Scotland Street) down to Allen Street, but there are few, if any, buildings remaining from the late nineteenth century.

CHAPTER 26

THE BLOODY SUICIDE OF A SHEFFIELD BREWER, SHOREHAM STREET, 1891

'On arriving at the brewery, his actions led everyone to believe that he was not in his right mind'

The *Sheffield and Rotherham Independent* of June 20, 1891, carried a report of the death of Mr Henry Tomlinson, proprietor of the Anchor Brewery, Sheffield, which at the time was one of the largest in the region:

SUICIDE OF MR. HENRY TOMLINSON.

A FIERCE STRUGGLE.

Mr Henry Tomlinson, proprietor of the Anchor Brewery, Cherry Street, Sheffield, committed suicide yesterday by cutting his throat. The circumstances under which the rash act was committed are both tragic and sad. For some time past Mr Tomlinson's condition has caused grave anxiety to his family and friends as it was becoming increasingly evident that he was suffering from mania, and it was suspected that he might either injure himself or those about him. As it turns out, it is a pity he was not placed under restraint, but perhaps his mental condition scarcely justified so extreme a step. The precaution, however, was taken of having him watched.

Mr Tomlinson resided at Woodlands, Dore New Road. He was in a restless and excited state during the whole of Thursday night, and at a very early hour yesterday morning one of his daughters called up Mr D. H. Porrett, who was his solicitor, and lives but a short distance off. Mr Porrett went to the Woodlands and remained with Mr Tomlinson for about three hours, during which time he was endeavouring to allay his excitement and to induce him to try to get some sleep. His well-meant actions were unfortunately not very successful. Mr Tomlinson left his house shortly after six o'clock and walked to Sheffield. A little before seven o'clock Inspector Thompson met him on the Abbeydale Road near the residence of Mr Henry Harrison. Mr Tomlinson bade him good morning, and Inspector Thompson says he did not observe there was anything unusual in his manner. Soon afterwards, Mr Tomlinson entered the Police Station at Highfield. Police Constable Dickinson, who was in charge of the station, noticed that he was in a most excited state, and that perspiration was almost rolling down his face. He told Dickinson that a lot of boys had been shouting at him, that he had murdered his wife and four children with his walking stick, and that he had thrown the stick after them. In a little time he became less excited, and said Mr Porrett and two men were coming in a cab to take him to a lunatic asylum.

'Tell them,' he added, that I don't want to have a crowd in the street; that they are to bring the cab down to the bottom of Woodhead Road and have the door wide open; I will then leave the brewery and walk straight into the cab, and they can take me right away to the asylum.' In the course of further conversation, he observed, 'They tell me I shall cut my throat; but see, I have shaved myself this morning and I haven't done that.' Dickinson asked him if he had a razor or knife about him, and he replied that he had not. He then pulled something from one of his pockets which was wrapped in paper, and said it was gold. Mr Tomlinson remained at the station for some time, and then went to his brewery, which is but a short distance off. He told the workmen whom he met there that several persons were trying to get hold of him, and he insisted on the brewery gates being closed to prevent their admission. After staying there till about nine o'clock he proceeded to the house of Mr Arthur Podgson, his confidential clerk and cashier, who resides at 327 Shoreham Street, and was accompanied thither by his groom, a young man named Charles Atkinson. He asked to have a cup of tea, and

after drinking it laid down on a sofa. His manner, however, was so strange that Mr Podgson considered it advisable to send for a doctor to ascertain whether he was insane. Dr Hardwicke came, but said it would be necessary to have a second surgeon before steps could be taken to remove him to an asylum, and it was arranged that Dr Hunt should also be called in.

Mr Podgson then left his house to consult with Mr George Tomlinson, the deceased's brother, as to the best course to be pursued. A few minutes afterwards Mr Tomlinson suddenly got up from the sofa and snatching a teaspoon from the breakfast table endeavoured to force it into his throat. Atkinson took it away from him, and then Mr Tomlinson got hold of a pair of sugar tongs, which he put against his throat and which Atkinson likewise took away. He then said, 'Lend me your knife.' Atkinson replied that he hadn't one, and added that his master didn't want a knife. 'Oh, yes I do,' said he; 'it's no use you keeping me here. I want to go out; let me go out.' He then said he should go into the kitchen, but Atkinson endeavoured to induce him to remain where he was, and stood in such a position as to prevent him getting there. He next made his way to the dining room, and thence walked sharply into the kitchen. Unfortunately there was a knife on the table. Mr Tomlinson instantly saw it and snatched it up. Atkinson was just behind him and immediately closed with him. A terrible struggle now ensued for possession of the knife, in which Mrs Podgson also took part. Unfortunately for Atkinson he was only able to get hold of the blade, but this he bravely held until at length, by sheer force, Mr Tomlinson succeeded in drawing it away. Atkinson sustained a most serious cut, extending from the thumb right across the hand below the fingers and reaching down to the bone. Blood flowed profusely from the wound, but he continued to struggle with his master till he became faint from loss of blood. He then gave up, and went to a neighbouring chemist's, to have the wound attended to.

As soon as Mr Tomlinson found himself free, he rushed from the kitchen into the scullery, and closed the door. A moment or two afterwards Mrs Podgson slightly opened the door and saw blood on the floor. She also heard Mr Tomlinson making what she described as a 'gurgling' sound. She then ran to the brewery for assistance, and on two men returning with her they discovered that Mr Tomlinson had cut his throat. Dr Hardwicke and Dr Hunt were promptly in attendance, but life was extinct. Death, indeed, must have taken place within a very short time after the wound was inflicted, for both the jugular vein and the windpipe were cut. The police were then communicated with, and Inspector Walsh took charge of the body, and had it removed to the mortuary.

The deceased, who was 46 years of age, was a son of the late Mr Tomlinson, of the Angel Hotel, Moorhead. He was formerly in partnership with Mr J. Richdale, and during the existence of the partnership the firm built the Britannia Brewery, in Bramall Lane. A few years ago the partnership was dissolved, and Mr Tomlinson subsequently erected the Anchor Brewery, and succeeded in establishing a flourishing business. He leaves a widow and four children – three daughters and one son, the latter being thirteen years of age.

No.327 Shoreham Street, Arthur Podgson's house, where Henry Tomlinson slit his own throat (photograph 2011)

Two days later the same newspaper gave a detailed report of the inquest into Tomlinson's death:

[Questioning Mr Podgson] The Coroner: 'Are you prepared to swear that, to the best of your opinion, the deceased was not in his right mind when you left him to go to his brother?'

'I am.'

[Questioning Charles Atkinson] The Coroner: 'What state of mind do you say that the deceased was in? You say he was very much excited?'

'Well, I don't think he was right, sir.'

'Was he in a habit of talking to himself?'

'No, I never heard him do it before.'

'You swear to the best of your belief, he was not in his right mind when he cut his throat?'

'I think he was not.'

The Coroner, addressing the jury, said Mr Porrett had brought Dr Hardwicke to give evidence if necessary, but he (the Coroner) did not think there was any necessity to ask him more than one question. (To Dr Hardwicke): 'You saw him before he died?'

'Yes.'

'What was your opinion of his state of mind then?

'I was of opinion that he was not responsible for his actions.'

'Is it a fact that you thought it a fit and proper case to send to an asylum?'

'Yes. Both Mr Podgson and I endeavoured for some time to persuade him to go home. But he declared he would not go, and persisted in saying that he wanted to go to an asylum. I, therefore, thought it would be advisable to take him at his word, and have him removed to a place where he could be kept quiet; but in order to do that I should require another medical man.'

'You still think you would have been justified in putting him under control somewhere?'

'Certainly, for the time being,'

The Coroner, addressing the jury, said this was conclusive as to what the deceased's state of mind was. He did not propose to call any further evidence. Here was a poor fellow who, from one cause or another, got into such a mental condition that he cut his throat in such a way as to result in his death. He did not want to go into the case more than was necessary in order to enable the jury to discharge their duty. The jury, without any hesitation, brought in a verdict that the deceased committed suicide whilst in a state of temporary insanity.

It was not mentioned at the inquest, but Tomlinson had previously engaged in odd behaviour, some fourteen years earlier, which may have been an indication as to his state of mind. In March 1877 the *Sheffield and Rotherham Independent* reported that Tomlinson had appeared in *Nisi Prius* Court, defending himself against an accusation of assaulting Mr Frank Fenton at the Beauchief Railway Hotel. According to the report, Tomlinson had 'without having received any provocation struck off plaintiff's hat'. A fight ensued, during which Fenton suffered a broken finger, adversely affecting his capacity to conduct his business, for which he was seeking compensation. Fenton was awarded the sum of £5, with both plaintiff and defendant paying their own costs. It was also revealed in court that a year earlier Tomlinson had assaulted another man, named Burton, after a disagreement over a drink.

Henry Tomlinson's home, 'The Woodlands', was in the village of Dore, which in 1891 was quite separate from the then town of Sheffield. It was a lengthy walk he undertook that June morning to his brewery a mile or so from the centre of town. He lived with his wife Martha, aged 44, son William (15) and daughter Dorothy (14). Henry and Martha married in 1865.

Douglas Lamb's book *A Pub On Every Corner* states that the Anchor Brewery was set up by Tomlinson in 1891, but considering that its owner died in June of that year and had already 'succeeded in establishing a flourishing business', it seems unlikely that he had been able to do so in just six months. The Anchor Brewery was situated on Cherry Street, opposite the Sheffield United football ground. It was bomb damaged in 1940 and in 1942 merged with the Hope Brewery, Claywheels Lane, to form the Hope and Anchor Brewery. This was taken over by Truswell's brewery in 1954 and subsequently Bass Charrington in 1963. Some of the old Anchor Brewery offices were used for many years by the Arnold Laver timber group, before the site was sold for apartments in the 2000s, up to which time the brewery's anchor insignia could still be seen on a wall on Cherry Street. It is now a residential development, named 'Anchor Point', which is a nice nod to history. The Britannia brewery, in which Tomlinson was formerly a partner, was where the petrol station now stands on Bramall Lane, between the church and the football ground.

The Anchor Point residential development on the corner of Bramall Lane and Cherry Street, once the site of the Anchor Brewery. In the foreground is the car park of the Copthorne Hotel (photograph 2011).

The Ship Inn, Shalesmoor, a rare, perhaps unique, surviving example of a Tomlinson's pub, with its 'Anchor Brewery' insignia

CHAPTER 27

A FATAL DOMESTIC ARGUMENT AT WALKLEY, 1899

'I banged her head against the wall and she fell down upon the floor'

On May 15, 1899, the *Sheffield and Rotherham Independent* reported:

SENSATIONAL AFFAIR AT WALKLEY.

FATAL ASSAULT ON A WIFE.

"BANGED HER HEAD AGAINST THE WALL."

The quiet neighbourhood of Daniel Hill, Walkley, was on Saturday evening the scene of a tragedy of a more painful nature than any that has recently occurred in Sheffield – as painful in its circumstances, more painful in the fact that it had a fatal result which, happily, has been wanting in the other affairs of violence that we have lately had to chronicle. Samuel Holroyd, a French polisher, going home and finding his wife drunk, assaulted her and she died, probably not entirely because of the injuries inflicted by his blows, but also because the enfeebled state to which intoxication brought her, rendered her more liable to succumb to violence. The crime of causing his wife's death with which Holroyd is now charged, appears to have been free from all premeditation, and for a murder – if is has to be called such – it shows a remarkable absence of those ghastly details which usually contribute towards the shocking effect of such occurrences. The fact that it was witnessed by no one probably accounts for the little excitement which it has caused. Few people in the neighbourhood seemed to know last night that there had been a fatal quarrel in their midst.

No particulars of that quarrel are available, except those supplied by Holroyd himself, who, when taken into custody and warned in the usual way, made a statement as to all that happened. From this appears that about half-past four on Saturday afternoon, he went to his home – 2, Yeoman's Road, off Cleveland Street – and found no one in but his wife, who was drunk. He remonstrated with her for being 'on the old racket again', and felt in the bosom of her dress to see if she had her watch, as she often pawned it when the craving for drink was upon her. He could not find the watch, and, perhaps fearing that he might strike her, his wife went from the living room, where they were, into the front room. He followed her, and she tried to shut the door and keep him out, but he pushed his way in. 'I pushed her,' says Holroyd, 'and slapped her face, then I banged her head against the wall and she fell down upon the floor. I let her lie and went to get the tea ready. After about ten minutes I went to her to wake her up, and poured some water on her face, but she took no notice of it. I then saw she was bad, and went and fetched Dr Hudson, but when he arrived she was dead. She still lay in the same position that she did when I left her.' The husband added that his wife had been a great drinker for years, and had caused him much trouble, and concluded by declaring, 'I did not mean to kill her.' When he was taken into custody, and told that he must be charged with causing her death, he replied, 'All right.'

But little can be gathered in addition to what Holroyd says. He is a man of 50 years of age, and his wife is 45, and they have been married about 24 years. The brightness of a happy married life seems in their case to have been continually obscured by the baneful shadow of intemperance, and there appears only too much reason to believe that the trouble has been of her causing. When she was sober, those who knew them declare they lived happily together, but for years he has *been addicted to drink, and has often been more or less drunk for weeks at a time. Before Saturday, she had been drunk off and on for a fortnight. The man's statement that she pawned things in order to get money for drink is also confirmed. He, on the other hand, is described as a steady man, quiet, and one who, though it is about twelve months since he removed from Nottingham Street and went to live in Yeomans Road, has made no acquaintances among his neighbours. He lived in his own house, and some of the adjoining ones are also his property, for he was in a comfortable position, having carried on business for himself as a French polisher in Corporation Street for almost 30 years. They had three sons, the eldest being nearly 21 years of age, and working with his father, the other boys being of twelve and six respectively. None of these were in on Saturday afternoon, though the two younger ones were playing not far away. The elder of the two had seen his mother about three o'clock, and she was not sober then. No one, so far as we have learned, saw Holroyd enter the house, and the quarrel between the man and his wife did not attract the attention of any of his neighbours.*

The people living next door, at a house which fronts Cleveland Street, thought they had heard some knocking, but they took little notice of it. Though they knew little of the parties, they were aware of the woman's habits, and thought that this was but another of the ordinary quarrels which frequently took place. It is known that Holroyd, who had tried all in his power to reform his wife, had at times used threats instead of persuasion, and it will probably be found that he had been violent as well. At any rate, the knocking attracted no attention, and Holroyd himself was the first to give information of his wife's state. He went, as he says, to Dr Hudson, who lives in Montgomery Terrace Road, and asked him to come and see his wife. Afterwards, he was asked if she was not dead when he left the house, but he said she was not, as he heard her rambling just before he called her, and then she suddenly became quiet. At all events, the injuries proved fatal in a very short time. She was dead when the doctor arrived, and he could do nothing but go back to his surgery and telephone to the police. Holroyd was calm, and his eldest son, Harold, who had come home about six o'clock, was in the house with him. Police Sergeant Jeeves received the information, and got to the house shortly before seven o'clock. He found father and son together, and the father made no attempt to get away, but quietly made his statement and allowed himself to be taken into custody. He was quite sober.

When an examination was made of the dead body, it was found that there were two wounds on the back of the head. One, about three inches long, and of a considerable depth, was a jagged cut, on the right side, slanting upwards; the other was about an inch and a quarter in length, and a straight cut. The place where the woman's head had come into contact with the wall was shown by a large patch of blood on the paper darker in two particular spots than elsewhere, and seeming to indicate that she had been banged against the wall more than once. This was about four feet high, and she appeared to have been knocked over a chair, which stood just in front of the patch. Then she had fallen to the floor, a slanting streak of blood showing that her head had held to the wall during the fall, and by her head on the floor was a pool of blood. The patch of blood on the wall measured about a foot across. The furniture in the room was not disturbed.

As to the cause of death, that will best be given in the words of Dr H. L. Hudson, who was seen by our reporter. He said that Holroyd went to his surgery on Saturday afternoon, and asked him to come and see his wife. Holroyd was evidently greatly troubled, but his behaviour was quite rational, and there was nothing unusual in his manner. He told the doctor that he had gone home, and had found his wife drunk, and that he had been 'hitting' her. The doctor, however, was quite surprised when he reached Holroyd's house, and found the woman lying on the floor between the kitchen and the sitting room, quite dead. The wounds in themselves were not sufficient to cause death, and the exact cause of death could not be known until a post-mortem examination had been made. The most common cause of death was haemorrhage on the brain.

Ten days later the same newspaper published a report of Holroyd's appearance in front of the Sheffield magistrates:

THE WALKLEY TRAGEDY
PRISONER CHARGED WITH MURDER
A PETITION WITH A THOUSAND SIGNATURES
In the Police Court of the city of Sheffield, yesterday, before the Stipendiary Magistrate, Mr E. M. E. Welby, Samuel Holroyd, French polisher, of 2, Yeomans Road, Walkley, was charged with the murder of his wife, Ellen Holroyd, on May 13th. Prisoner, who was dressed in mourning, was allowed to have a chair placed in the dock. Mr Ernest W. Clegg prosecuted for the Treasury, and the defence was conducted by Mr A. Neal.

Mr Clegg explained the circumstances of the case, before Harold Holroyd, eldest son of the prisoner, was called to give evidence. He saw his mother at eight o'clock in the morning, but could not say whether or not she was drunk. He returned home about six o'clock to find his father standing over the body of his mother. He told the court that his mother was his father's second wife, and he was a child of this marriage. She was a kind and affectionate wife and mother when she was sober, and his father was very much attached to her. However, she had been addicted to severe drinking for a number of years and her drinking bouts varied from a fortnight to five weeks. When she was drunk she was almost uncontrollable, falling about and hurting herself, and his father had done his best to break her habit. Prior to May 13 she had been drinking for about two weeks. When she was drinking his father kept money from her, so she pawned property to enable her to buy drink. One item she frequently pawned was a watch, formerly owned by her mother. Efforts had been made to keep her in the house but once she escaped through a window, another time through a cellar grate. He said he did not think it would have been easier for his mother to make her way out of the back door, when the scuffle took place in the kitchen, than into the front room. His father very seldom spoke to his wife about her drunkenness. Harold's younger brother Laurence then stated that his mother was drunk at two o'clock in the afternoon of May 13.

The next witness was Dr Herbert Leonard Hudson. He gave evidence that he had been called to the house by Holroyd, who told him that his wife was drunk, he had hit her, and he was afraid she had fainted. Hudson estimated that when he arrived at the house she had been dead about half an hour. He told Holroyd that the matter might be very serious for him, to which the prisoner replied, 'I can't help it if it is.' Holroyd led Hudson to infer that his life had been made miserable by his wife's drunkenness, and did not care what happened to him. The doctor then gave details of the woman's injuries, stating that merely falling against a wall would not have caused them, but a violent push against the wall would have done so. In his opinion there had been two such pushes.

The report then detailed an exchange between Dr Hudson and Mr Neal:

Mr Neal: 'Are you prepared to swear that the woman died from the injuries?'

Witness: 'I am prepared to say she died as a result of her injuries.'

Mr Neal: 'That is the same thing. You are – think before you answer. I do not want to press you unduly or unfairly; but are you prepared to swear she died as a result of those injuries?'

Witness: 'I am prepared to swear that is my opinion.' Mr Neal then read from the doctor's evidence at the inquest. 'Did you, in point of fact, find anything sufficient to account for death?' 'No, I cannot say I did,' and he asked witness if that was correct. Dr Hudson replied that it was, but he must qualify it.

Mr Neal: 'Did you, not finding anything to account for death, use the generic term, and say that shock was the cause of death?'

Witness: 'Yes.'

Mr Neal: 'Before the coroner did you also say, I think perfectly fairly, that death may have resulted from a natural stoppage of the heart's action caused by excitement?'

Witness: 'You suggested that and I said it was possible.'

Mr Neal: 'Did you find from post-mortem examination evidence of the fact that the deceased was an intemperate woman?'

Witness: 'I did.'

By other questions, Mr Neal ascertained that the height of the deceased woman was 5ft 5in, and the bloodstains on the wall were too low to have been caused by the head of a person of that height who was standing erect, being banged against the wall, and if the deceased had been sitting in a chair which stood by the door, and had her head banged against the wall the blood marks would not have been so high as most of those which were on the wall.

Mr Neal: 'Now doctor, assume that Mr Holroyd had pushed his wife violently backwards towards the chair, that she had lost her balance and her head had come in contact with the wall, and that then she had slipped downwards, with her head on the wall, into the chair, might that not account for the bloodstain on the wall?'

Witness: 'It might. It is not likely.'

Nr Neal: 'Perhaps not. Unlikely things happen. But the position of the stain on the wall favours that, does it not?'

Witness: 'Yes.'

Mr Neal: 'Assuming, again, that there had been a struggle in the little kitchen for the possession of a watch which the woman had in the bosom of her dress, and that she had been forced backwards with her head against the sink, might that account for the other wound?'

Witness: 'Yes, providing, as I said at the inquest, her head came into sufficiently violent contact with the sinkstone.'

In re-examination, witness said he thought that probably there had been two bangs of the deceased's head against the wall.

Sergeant Jeeves was then called, and repeated the prisoner's statement to him. He said he had examined the kitchen, including the sinkstone and the wringing machine. There were no blood marks anywhere in the room, and there was no appearance of a struggle having taken place there. The *Independent* report then continued:

Mr Neal, addressing the Stipendiary, asked him to carefully consider whether there was any case on which to send prisoner for trial for manslaughter.

The Stipendiary: 'The charge is murder.' Mr Neal said he did not want to be disrespectful to a Treasury prosecution, but that seemed utterly ridiculous.

Mr Clegg: 'At the present moment the charge of murder stands without any abatement.'

Mr Neal: 'Then I shall ask you, sir, to dismiss the charge of murder against the prisoner, for anything more ridiculous than to charge Mr Holroyd with the wilful murder of his wife on this evidence I cannot imagine.'

The Stipendiary: 'The charge of murder has gone a long way.'

Mr Neal: 'It has, sir, but it has not gone so far as this, that a man who commits a common assault, and in that common assault kills, can be committed for murder. That charge could only be if the man committed a felony, when the law transfers one felony to the other.'

Mr Neal added that if a burglar, who never had any intention of killing anybody, did kill a person in the process of his burglary, the law transferred the felonious intent from the burglary to the killing, and called it murder.

The Stipendiary: 'He is in the committal of an unlawful act.'

Mr Neal: 'With great respect, I think it must be a felonious act.'

The Stipendiary said that the charge was murder, and there was some evidence of what might be called a technical murder. If the Coroner's jury thought it was a very serious charge of manslaughter, he agreed with them. Mr Neal said the foreman of the jury had told him the jury considered it a case of accidental death. The Stipendiary said he could not agree with that. He thought it was a serious case of manslaughter.

Mr Neal: 'Then I understand you intend to commit for manslaughter?'

The Stipendiary said he could not say. If the prosecution insisted on their charge there was evidence of a technical murder. Mt Neal said that in the first place there was no evidence that the prisoner caused the death. The doctor said he was not prepared to swear to the cause of death, and was not prepared to swear that the woman did not die from stoppage of the heart's action. By the post-mortem examination he found no evidence sufficient to account for death. Surely his Worship would not say there was a tittle of evidence on which Mr Holroyd could be sent for trial on a charge exceeding manslaughter. Murder was feloniously killing with malice aforethought. Where was the evidence of that? There was no scrap of evidence against Mr Holroyd more than his own statement that he banged her head.

The Stipendiary: 'What business has he, in point of law, to bang her head?'

Mr Neal: 'None.'

Mr Neal proceeded to review the facts of the case, and he added that he had had brought with him a petition from prisoner's neighbours in Nottingham Street, signed by 1075 persons. (Applause.)

The Stipendiary: 'If there is any more noise the court will be cleared.' The Stipendiary added that these people had no right to interfere with the law.

Mr Neal: 'But if you consider the reputation of the man.'

The Stipendiary: 'I have to deal with the facts.'

Mr Neal then appealed to the Stipendiary to send the prisoner for trial on the charge of manslaughter. The Stipendiary said that what Mr Neal had urged might be put before a jury. There was another aspect of the case which to his mind was more apparent. It was that this woman was unfortunately given to drinking habits, which evidently highly incensed her husband. On this occasion he may have been aggravated by some matter of the watch, and having lost control of himself and his temper, he banged her about in a way which, either directly or indirectly, resulted in her death. It was very difficult to deal with the difference between murder and manslaughter at a preliminary enquiry. If it had been left entirely to him he would have considered it a very serious case of manslaughter. He did not know whether the charge of murder was pressed. Mr Clegg said he did not wish to prosecute vindictively, and if there was an adjournment he would seek instructions from the Treasury as to reducing the charge. A remand was thereupon granted until Monday, with leave to bring the case forward on Friday if the Treasury instructions have been received by then.

The hearing resumed the following Monday, and was reported on by the *Sheffield and Rotherham Independent* on May 30:

HOLROYD'S CASE
CHARGE REDUCED TO MANSLAUGHTER
Samuel Holroyd, French polisher, 2, Yeomans Road, was again brought up in custody on the charge of murdering his wife, Ellen Holroyd, on May 13th. Mr E. W. Clegg appeared to prosecute for the Treasury, and Mr A. Neal represented prisoner. Mr Clegg said since Wednesday last he had received a letter from the Treasury, in which they stated they had no objection whatever to the charge being reduced to one of manslaughter.

Mr Neal: 'Then, sir, upon that I ask for bail. Defendant is able to offer substantial bail, and whatever your Worship thinks ought to be done in that respect can be done, I have no doubt.'

The Stipendiary (to Mr Clegg): 'Is anything said about bail?'

Mr Clegg: 'No, only I suggest it should be fixed in a very substantial amount. I think he will have no difficulty finding whatever you may fix.'

Mr Neal: 'I don't know – anything in reason. I would suggest two sureties of £100 each, and himself in £200. Mr Holroyd is a substantial property owner himself, and can find two sureties without the least difficulty.'

No objection was offered by Mr Clegg, and the Stipendiary allowed bail in the amount suggested.

Holroyd appeared at Leeds Assizes in late July. The jury was sympathetic to his circumstances, possibly because of his wife's excessive and constant drunkenness, and acquitted him even on the reduced charge of manslaughter. There is no question that manslaughter, not murder, was the correct charge, but on the evidence given at the various proceedings Holroyd could consider himself fortunate to be found not guilty of any offence.

No.2 Yeoman's Road, where the death of Ellen Holroyd occurred (it is the white house to the left – the larger house on the corner is No.23 Cleveland Street) (photograph 2012)

Montgomery Terrace Road, about a quarter of a mile from the scene, to where Samuel Holroyd ran to fetch Dr Hudson (photograph 2012)

CHAPTER 28

DROWNED PULLING A CAT ACROSS A CANAL, ATTERCLIFFE, 1899

'They all went to the bank together, Claytor bringing his cat'

On May 25, 1899, the *Sheffield and Rotherham Independent* reported an unusual fatal accident that occurred at Attercliffe the previous day:

MAN DROWNED AT ATTERCLIFFE.

THE SEQUEL TO A FOOLISH PRACTICAL JOKE.

Early yesterday morning, as the outcome of the common and foolish practical joke of 'pulling a cat across water', a man, named George Jones, was drowned in the canal at Attercliffe. Notwithstanding the number of drowning cases which have been caused by this absurd and dangerous prank, there are many who have never heard of the practice, and are simple enough to take the wager in which it originates. In most cases nowadays the prank is not played, or even attempted to be played

163

on any man until he is well under the influence of drink, and it rarely happens that sober men perpetrate the so-called joke. In the present case the victim, who was 40 years of age, and who lodged with William Henry Jinks at 18, Elbury Street, Attercliffe, has not been working for some days, and since Friday night several of his pot-house companions have been chaffing him, and telling him that he could not pull a cat across the canal at Attercliffe. This chaffing was kept up, especially when it was seen that Jones did not know the trick, and would be a likely victim. The upshot was that, while Jones was in the Golden Ball Hotel, Attercliffe, towards 10 o'clock yesterday morning, along with several others, including a man named Thomas Gerrard, of 44, Old Hall Road, after considerable talking of pulling a cat over the water, a bet for half a gallon of beer was made between Jones and Gerrard that the former could not pull a cat across the canal close to the Great Central Station, Attercliffe. Jones, after making the bet, went to fetch his landlord, Jinks, to watch him perform the feat, while another of the men, John Claytor, went to fetch his cat, and Gerrard got a rope.

The party then repaired to the chosen spot, where there soon congregated several onlookers besides those who intended to aid the cat. Jones was not quite so foolish as he at first appeared, for he took with him a pick shaft, which he evidently intended to aid him in keeping his footing. Gerrard was on the same side with him as well as Claytor, and when it was seen that Jones intended to use the pick, Gerrard and some of his companions demurred. Jones refused to have the noose on the rope fastened round his body, and an argument ensued, as a result of which Claytor refused to have anything further to do with the matter, and took his cat away. Gerrard then declared he had won the bet, and pressed Jones for payment. The latter refused to pay, and, in fact, had only a halfpenny on him. Gerrard threatened to duck Jones in the canal unless he paid. He seized Jones, apparently intending to carry out his threat. Both men struggled on the bank and eventually fell together into the water, Jones undermost. A rope was thrown to the struggling men, which Gerrard managed to catch, and by which he was drawn to the bank and helped out, but in the meantime Jones sank to the bottom and was drowned. One of the onlookers, Thomas Belk, of Darnall Road, plunged into the water to recover the body but failed to find it. About the same time a barge passed the spot, and one of the boatmen, whose name has not been ascertained, recovered the body by means of a boat hook, some ten yards away from where Jones entered the water. The body was afterwards removed to the mortuary, Plum Lane, to await a coroner's inquest. Jones, who is supposed to have come from Shropshire, was a single man, who had been employed as a navvy by Mr Carr on some work at Fir Vale. Afterwards Gerrard went home and went to bed to wait for his clothes to dry.

After the occurrence, William Henry Jinks, puddler, of 18, Elbury Street, furnished some details of the affair. George Jones and Jinks lodged together at the address given above. Jones had not been working since Saturday. About nine o'clock he came home, and calling to Jinks, who was in bed, asked him to come downstairs. When Jinks reached the living room, Jones told him he was going to pull a cat across the canal, and invited him to assist in the ceremony. They went together to the Golden Ball Hotel, Attercliffe Road, when they found Gerrard, Claytor, and two or three others. Claytor had a cat. They all went to the bank together, Claytor bringing his cat. Jones, Gerrard, Claytor, and many others went up the steps at Attercliffe (G.C.R.) Station as though they were going to catch a train for Sheffield. When half way up the steps they got through the railings on to the canal side. Jones had a pick shaft with him, which he put through the rail fencing, so that he could hold fast to it while pulling the cat across. Those on the opposite bank shouted out that that would not be fair. Claytor then went away with his cat. The rope was not thrown across at that time. Gerrard and Jones got hold of each other, and fell into the water together. A rope was thrown to them, and Gerrard, getting hold of it, was pulled out, but Jones was drowned. When the two men fell into the water Jones was underneath. Both men were, it is said, under the influence of drink

Thomas Gerrard was arrested and was twice brought before the Stipendiary Magistrate, Mr E. M. E. Welby, on a charge of the manslaughter of George Jones. The *Sheffield and Rotherham Independent* reported the events of the second hearing on May 30:

THE ATTERCLIFFE CANAL TRAGEDY
GERRARD DISCHARGED
Thomas Gerrard, iron worker, of 44, Old Hall Road, Attercliffe, again appeared before the Stipendiary Magistrate, this morning, the charge against him being one of manslaughter, arising out of the 'practical joking' affair at Attercliffe last week, through which a man named George Jones lost his life.

Since the case had last been before the Court the inquest on Jones had been held, and a verdict of 'Accidental Death' returned. Chief

Detective Inspector Moody informed the Stipendiary that it was not proposed to offer any evidence against Gerrard, and asked that he should be discharged. The Stipendiary assented, and Gerrard left the Court.

The canal near the former Attercliffe railway station. The railway line crosses the canal over the bridge in the background (photograph 2010)

The decision not to pursue the charge of manslaughter against Gerrard was understandable, as it did appear to be a drunken prank that had gone wrong. What is not explained in any of the reports, however, is exactly what 'pulling a cat across a canal' entailed, and why it was perceived to be so difficult. One can picture the frightened furry creature with a rope around its neck, battling frantically for its life as a man, the worse for drink, attempted to drag it from one side to the other. At least in this instance, even though a poor man met his death, the helpless animal survived to see another day, perhaps with only eight lives remaining.

CHAPTER 29

A CATASTROPHIC BOILER EXPLOSION, DONCASTER STREET, 1899

'Three bodies, mangled by fallen brickwork, blackened with ashes, reddened with blood, and swollen with scalds, were lying near together'

In December 2011 Chris Hobbs was asked if he had any information regarding an explosion in Sheffield in 1899 in which one of the correspondent's ancestors was killed. It turned out to be one of the most horrific accidents in the history of the city, resulting in multiple fatalities. The *Sheffield and Rotherham Independent* reported the incident on November 2, 1899:

BOILER DISASTER IN SHEFFIELD.

TERRIBLE DEATHS.

SEVEN KILLED: MANY INJURED.

Marvellous Escapes.

Yesterday morning a terribly disastrous boiler explosion occurred at the works of Messrs Southern and Richardson, cutlery manufacturers, Doncaster Street, Sheffield. The power for driving the grinding wheels and other machinery in the works was provided by a large Lancashire boiler, built between two blocks of shops. The boiler was an old one, nearly, if not quite, at the end of its usefulness. Many times it had been 'patched up', but the firm had realised it was practically 'done' for, and in a few weeks' time it would have been entirely dispensed with, a powerful gas engine having already been purchased to take its place. Yesterday's most lamentable accident has put an end to the boiler's existence as a boiler in a terribly tragic manner. There was a few minutes' warning of impending danger in the shape of a leakage into one of the flues, and then with a roar like that of heavy artillery the explosion took place. It was an explosion down into one of the flues, and the effects were horizontal in two directions. At one end the fire plate was blown off, two occupants of the fire hole being instantly killed, and at the other the brickwork of the chamber which diverts the heated gases from the flues to the smoke stack, was hurled across a yard into the goffing shop and a number of men and boys working there were injured by flying debris and scalding steam and water. All the surrounding workshops were instantly filled with steam, and while some of the workmen stampeded, others, realising that their means of escape was cut off, smashed the windows of their workshops and lay down upon the floor until the steam became less suffocating.

The steam hung about the damaged boiler and the workshops for about a quarter of an hour, but within a much shorter time than that it was possible to ascertain in some degree the extent of the catastrophe. In the fire hole there were found three bodies – those of the boiler tenter, whose name was Lickfold; of the caretaker, named Dickinson; and of a cutler, named William Ward. It was a ghastly spectacle which the steaming fire hole presented, and one which gave some idea of the force of the explosion. A pathway leading to an entrance in Ellis Street had skirted the pit of the fire hole, and beyond the pathway and within a very few yards of the boiler front there was a wall. The explosion had torn the iron fire plate from its fastenings, ripped up the pathway, and tumbled down the brickwork of the wall. Whether there were two or three men in the fire hole at the actual moment of the explosion is not quite clear. It is said that Ward was in one of the cutlers' shops at the time, and that he rushed down a staircase with the evident intention of trying to escape by the pathway near the boiler front. If he did so he probably ran blindly into the stream of hot water and steam which was pouring into the fire hole at the time. When found the three bodies, mangled by fallen brickwork, blackened with ashes, reddened with blood, and swollen with scalds, were lying near together. At the other end of the boiler the effects of the explosion were hardly less distressing, and while yet the steam hung around, a sickening chorus of moans told a story of tragic portent in this direction.

The 'goffing shop' being directly opposite the boiler, at a few yards distance, naturally suffered greatly. Four of the six men at work there were fatally hurt. The shop is close to Doncaster Street, with which it communicates by a window, and there is a doorway into the yard. The shop is divided into two compartments, in each of which is a 'goffing' hammer, and a small fire for heating the bars of iron which is 'goffed' into blades. That nearest the yard, which is slightly below the ground level, is lighted by a sort of grating. At the time of the accident the shop was fully at work. A man was manipulating each of the hammers, and a vertical stamper was also in use. Three boys were engaged at the fires and in other ways. The tremendous force of the explosion sent a deadly shower of steam and bricks into the shop. Everyone in the place was injured more or less by the falling missiles and the steam and two of the youths, Wharton and Anderson, were so badly hurt that they died, one on the way to and the other at the Infirmary. A sixth death, that of a man named Whitehead, who was also employed in the 'goffing' shop, occurred in the evening, and a seventh, that of John Ellis, was announced a little later. Pools of water a couple of feet deep were left in some parts of the shop, but curiously enough the machinery was little damaged.

It is hardly necessary to say that the news of the explosion spread with the rapidity with which ill news always travels. The goffing shop window was blown out into Doncaster Street, and the sound of the concussion was heard far and wide. A crowd quickly gathered, and when information as to the killed and injured filtered through to the street there were some distressing scenes, women and children becoming hysterical in their grief. The work of removing the dead and injured was undertaken by the police, and by a detachment of the Fire Brigade under Superintendent Frost. The dead were removed to the mortuary, and the injured to the Royal Infirmary, the ambulances of the police, the Fire Brigade, and those from the works of Messrs Cammell and John Brown and Co. being requisitioned for this purpose. The works were to have been closed at noon yesterday for the funeral, in the afternoon, of Mr Shimmels, one of the managers, but of course work ceased with the explosion. Some of the workmen went home, but others lingered about the premises and talked in subdued tones of this disaster, and of the circumstances which had immediately preceded it. A grinder, employed in a shop quite close to the firing end of the boiler, gave a graphic account of all that had happened that morning so far as he was concerned. 'Between nine and ten o'clock,' he said, 'we heard that there was a leakage in one of the tubes over the fire-box, and we went round to look at it. It was leaking very badly, and the engine tenter, a young man who only came here on Monday to take the place of a man who was sacked on Saturday, was considering what to do. It was agreed not to fire up any more, and then the manager, Mr Brant, came. There were about fifteen of us there at the time, and Mr Brant sent us all away to the shops, and he went away too. We had hardly got back to the shop, and my next door neighbour was saying to me that it wasn't very safe to be where we were when up she goes. The tenter and Dickinson, poor fellows, were sitting in the fire hole at the time talking about what was best to be done. The explosion made a noise which seemed to bung our ears up for the moment, and then the steam came into our shop and we could hardly breathe. There were eleven men and lads altogether in the shop. In a minute or two the engines stopped, and then we broke through an opening where the machinery had been running a couple of minutes before and got out into Shepherd Street. The cutlers in the shop above us had managed to get out before us, but one of them, William Ward, was found in the fire hole with Dickinson and the boiler tenter. He was a pocket-blade grinder, and when the men in his room hurried out they turned to the right and went through the engine house. But Ward turned to the left, came down the steps close to the boiler, and got caught in the steam I suppose. It was a terrible sight, both in the fire hole and the goffing shop. I saw one man whose head had been cut open by a brick, and lots of them were scalded. It's an awful thing, but it might have been much worse. If it had happened five minutes earlier all the fifteen of us would have been killed, and if it had happened on Monday when a lot of men were fixing the new gas engine it would have been all up with every one of them.'

The boiler is an ordinary Lancashire boiler, and was manufactured by the well-known Sheffield firm of Hawksley, Wild and Co. It is 28 feet long and seven feet in diameter. There are two parallel flues, in the right of which the explosion took place. The boiler was put down in 1875, and has been in use for 25 years. This, it may be remarked, is a full lifetime for a boiler of this description. The boiler was capable of generating an extreme power of 70lbs, but we understand that the firm used it so as to 'blow off' at 60lbs pressure. It was working at 60lbs pressure when the accident occurred yesterday. The water used was not taken from the Corporation mains but from a well on the premises. This may be a very important factor in the explanation of the causes of the explosion. Sheffield well water is, as is well known, heavily charged with ochre, and lime, and other matter, which are regularly deposited on the plates inside the boiler. This necessitates frequent cleaning of the inside. As the deposit eats into the metal, every fresh cleaning means a thinning away of the plates where a deposit has been. The result of this on the inside of the boiler is that 'pits' or depressions are left where the deposit has been cleared away, and the strength of the boiler to resist pressure is proportionately lessened.

The dead men were: Harry Dickinson, aged 55, caretaker; William Ward, aged 27, 8 court, 1 house, Bath Street; Herbert Arthur Lickfold, aged 24; Albert Wharton, aged 15, 71, Burnt Tree Lane; John Whitehead, aged 54, 26 Shepherd Street; Frank Anderson, aged 15, 4 court, 3 house, Burnt Tree Lane; John Ellis, aged 40, carter, in the employ of Messrs Doncaster and Sons. The injured were treated at the Infirmary. The most seriously hurt were: William Benn, of 13 court, 1 house, Hoyle Street and William Hibbert, aged 16, of 30 Brownhill Street.

An inquest was opened and adjourned to allow further investigations to take place. It resumed on November 23 and was reported the following day in the *Sheffield and Rotherham Independent*:

THE SHEFFIELD BOILER EXPLOSION - RESUMED INQUEST
A DEFECTIVE WATER GAUGE
The inquest on the bodies of the seven victims of the terrible boiler explosion which occurred on November 1st at the works of Messrs Southern and Richardson, cutlery manufacturers, Doncaster Street, was resumed yesterday by the City Coroner, Mr Dossey Wightman. The inquiry was held at the City Court House. Mr Edward G. Hiller, chief engineer and manager of the National Boiler and General Insurance Company, Manchester, was present at the inquiry, assisting the Coroner. Commander Hamilton Smith, Chief Inspector of Factories for the Sheffield district, was present, representing the Home Office. The firm of Southern and Richardson was represented by Mr Shepherd, of Leeds (instructed by Messrs Rodgers, Thomas and Sandford); Mr S. N. Hurd represented the Ocean Accident Insurance Company; Mr J. H.

Davidson represented Messrs Hattersley and Davidson, by whom the deceased man Lickfold, the engine tenter, was formerly employed; and Mr A. Neal represented the relatives of Ellis, who was employed by Messrs Daniel Doncaster and Sons, but happened to be on the premises at the time of the accident. Mr G. W. Hawksley, of Messrs Hawksley, Wild, and Co., by whom the boiler was supplied, was also present. Mr F. S. H. Wilson was foreman of the jury.

The first witness was Mr Samuel Gray Richardson, who said he was the sole proprietor of the Don Cutlery Works, Doncaster Street, and traded under the name of Southern and Richardson. The boiler which exploded was purchased by him from Messrs Hawksley, Wild, and Co. in 1875, and had been in constant use ever since. It was insured, and had been insured since 1883 in different companies. He could not find any policy dated previous to that, but it was his impression that it was insured soon after it was put down. Since 1885, it had been insured in the Engine Boiler Employers' Liability Insurance Corporation Limited. It had been regularly inspected by one of their inspectors every year, with the exception of once, when the inspector was ill. That was at the end of 1895. The exterior had been inspected much more than once a year. The insurance company were allowed to inspect it when and as they thought fit. He produced a report of the last inspection, which was made at Christmas, 1898. There was only one boiler in the works. The Saturday before the explosion, a boiler tenter named Stafford, who had been in the situation since last Easter, left his employment. When he came, Stafford was recommended to him by Tasker's Engineering Company as a thoroughly capable man.

The Coroner: 'Why did he leave your employment?

Witness: 'I was not satisfied with him altogether, and circumstances occurred on Thursday which caused me to think it desirable to have a change.'

The Coroner: 'Was it anything connected with the accident?'

Witness replied in the negative, and went on to explain that on Thursday afternoon one of the grinders came across to the office to say some pieces had broken out of his stone. Subsequently, witness learned that for the last two or three weeks the engine had been set to run faster than it used to do. He telephoned to Hattersley and Davidson's to send a man up at once, and explained to them that it would be better it should be set slower rather than have it too fast. In the meantime,

Stafford was told not to leave the place, but to keep his eye upon the engine. The table knife manager, some time afterwards, found, on going to the engine house, that he was not there, and saw him afterwards in the street. It was ascertained that the breaking of the stone had nothing whatever to do with the running of the engine, but owing to the fact that Stafford had gone away from the engine house when told not to do so, and that he seemed to think he knew more about the engine than he (Mr Richardson) or the representative of Messrs Hattersley and Davidson, witness thought it advisable that he should go.

Stafford would have left under any circumstances when the gas engine was put down. Afterwards witness spoke to Mr Davidson, and asked him to supply him with a man in Stafford's place. He sent the deceased Herbert Lickfold, who entered upon his duties on the Monday morning, Stafford having received a week's wages in lieu of notice. From half-past twelve to one on Saturday the caretaker took charge of the engine, Lickfold did not before the explosion tell him anything about the state of the boiler, or make any complaint about it. The only time witness saw him on duty was on Tuesday afternoon, when he said everything was going all right. Lickfold had sole charge of the boiler from the time he came until the explosion. When the explosion occurred, witness was on his way down to business.

By Mr Shepherd: 'Is it true that you decided to give up this boiler because it was done for?'

'Absolutely untrue.'

'And that it was at the end of its period of usefulness?'

'There is not the slightest ground for anything of the kind. I have never had the faintest suspicion that there was anything the matter with the boiler – the thought had never crossed my mind.'

'Had you full confidence in Hattersley and Davidson, and their recommendation of Lickfold?'

'Yes, I think him now to have been an efficient man.'

'Was there also a man called Wright, from Hattersley and Davidson's, at the works on Monday morning?'

'Yes. Wright, who knew the cisterns and supply of the boiler, was sent to instruct Lickfold in the working of the place.'

'Will you explain what was exactly the state of things with regard to the purchase of this gas engine?'

'Well, for some time the steam engine has not been running satisfactorily. There was a very considerable amount of time lost, not in long periods, but in small, irritating stoppages, and I had been considering for some time the desirability of replacing it. I did not make up my mind for some time whether to put down a new steam engine, a gas engine, or an electric engine, but I decided this year in favour of a gas engine. I had had considerable trouble with the Corporation about blowing off the boiler into the sewers, and I had had to give strict orders that that was never to be done. The insurance people, on the other hand, said it was very desirable to do so. They said we should blow off the boiler occasionally to get rid of the sediment. That finally decided me in favour of a gas engine. The question of the boiler being nearly worn out did not enter into it at all. It was not nearly worn out.'

The Coroner: 'In this report from the Insurance Company who made the examination of the boiler at Christmas, and the original of which you produce, the Inspector says: "Remarks. The boiler is too dirty; scale. Too thick to make a satisfactory examination. Please urge removal of the same, and if possible to change the water which comes from a well." Is that a correct copy of the original report?'

Witness: 'Yes, I think so.'

'Did you take any steps at all after you got this report?'

'Yes. At the time the report was taken the boiler had not been properly cleaned. The men came in accordance with the arrangement, but owing to the Messrs Hawksley, Wild, and Co. being engaged with the boiler, the men who were cleaning were unable to make the progress they otherwise would. As a matter of fact, the boiler was being scaled three days after the inspector's report was sent in.'

Commander Hamilton Smith: 'The report of the Engine Boiler Employers' Liability Insurance Company here states that the boiler is too dirty.'

Witness: 'You had better have the report which came to me.'

'This appears to be the report made by the inspector to his own society. Was any other representation made to you that a satisfactory examination of the boiler had been made in December?'

'No.'

'I should like to ask whether, seeing that the inspector reported that a satisfactory examination had not been made, they urged you to allow them another opportunity of making a satisfactory examination?'

'No. Nothing of the kind. They referred to this matter of the scale, which had been removed before the report reached me.'

Mr Shepherd: 'Is it not the practice to periodically examine the inside of the boiler for the purpose of cleaning it out, and was not a thorough cleaning of the boiler effected every three months?'

Witness: 'Yes. At Christmas, Easter, Whitsuntide and August Bank Holiday. The scale was removed as far as possible.'

'This boiler would be thoroughly cleaned as late as the beginning of August before the accident?'

'Yes.'

William Stafford, engine tenter, said he had charge of the boiler from Easter week until last Saturday. Witness found no fault whatever with the boiler before he left. The water gauge was all right when he left. The last time he blew it off was at 11 o'clock on Saturday morning, two hours before he left. He was in the habit of blowing it off three or four times a day. There were two gauges, but one of them was out of order owing to the glass being broken.

By Mr Hurd: 'One gauge was as good as two.'

Mr Hiller: 'Did you ever take any steps to ascertain whether the passages of the water gauges were dirty or had scale in them or not?'

Witness: 'I never had the opportunity of doing so.'

'You could have unscrewed the small plug, could you not?'

'I did not think it was necessary. The gauge was working all right.'

Mr Shepherd: 'Were you there when the insurance company's inspector inspected on the last occasion?'

Witness: 'Yes.'

'On that occasion did the inspector adopt the method of unscrewing the water gauges and taking them apart?'

'No, sir.'

Mr Neal: 'Did you take any steps to have the broken gauge put right?'

'Yes, but I was waiting for another washer to make the joint right at the bottom.'

'Why didn't you get a washer, or ask for one?'

'Dickinson, the caretaker, was looking around to get me one.'

Commander Hamilton Smith read the recommendation contained in the report of the insurance company, dated December 31st, that 'the boiler should be thoroughly scaled from end to end at the first opportunity, if only for convenience of working.' He asked witness if he could say how soon that recommendation was carried out.

Witness: 'No, sir. I cannot. I only took charge after Easter. I understand a certain amount of cleaning was done at Easter, prior to my taking charge.'

'Since you went there has the boiler ever been thoroughly scaled from end to end?'

'Not since I have been there.'

A Juryman: 'At the time you left did you consider there was sufficient water in the boiler to work it properly?'

Witness: 'Yes.'

'During the time you were there had you any misgivings with regard to the boiler itself?'

'No.'

'You were perfectly satisfied in your own mind that the boiler was safe?'

'So far as I knew, it was.'

Mr Edward George Hiller, chief engineer of the National Boiler and General Insurance Company, Manchester, said the company had upwards of 20,000 boilers under their inspection. He read his report of an examination of the boiler, which he made at the request of the Coroner on the 20th inst. He found that the third ring of the right furnace had ruptured or torn across about half-way round, and the back portion of this ring of plate was bent over until the edge of the ruptured part was only a little distance above the bottom of the tube. A gap was thus caused, and it was through this gap that water and steam were expelled with such disastrous results. Apart from this ruptured plate the structure of the boiler proper was not injured. Inside the boiler the plates of the outside shell were covered with a varying thickness of incrustation, and at the water level there was a little evidence of greasy deposit. The flue tubes on the lower parts had a coating of rough scale of irregular thickness. All the various fittings were in order except the water gauges. The inspector's account of these was as follows:

'The boiler is equipped with two water gauges with a water level pointer between them. The left-hand water gauge was shut off at the time of my examination, and was out of use at the time of the explosion. I carefully examined the plugs and passages of the right-hand water gauge, which was the one depended on at the time of the explosion. All the plugs and waterways were free excepting the passage through the top fitting. In the top of this fitting I found that the small passage was perfectly choked up with incrustation. The passage between the plug and the boiler was also was also very nearly filled with incrustation. The result of this would be in actual working that when the boiler was working with a proper level of water it would gradually and slowly rise in this gauge glass until the gauge indicated correctly. When the water in the boiler, however, sank to a lower level owing to its being evaporated into steam and used in the engine, the water in the gauge glass would not fall, but would continue at the same level, and indicate that there was plenty of water in the boiler when the water was reaching a dangerously low level. The cause of the explosion was overheating, consequent on deficiency of water. The water gauge which was in use was not in good order, the top passage connecting the gauge glass to the steam space being chocked up. The consequence of this was that a misleading indication of the level of the water in the boiler was given. The water in the boiler was gradually evaporated into steam, and the water sank lower and lower in this way until the tops of the furnace tubes were bared. When this took place the fires inside the furnaces would begin to overheat the crowns of the tubes, and there is distinct evidence that this has been done in both tubes. Probably the overheating allowed some slight escape of steam such as the leakage which was noticed in the left furnace. Evidently the fire in the right-hand furnace had been much brighter than that in the left, and in a short time the right-hand furnace crown became red hot. The plate was so much weakened by becoming red hot that, although it was of a full thickness and a good plate, it ruptured across the middle and bent* *down to the bottom of the tube, resulting in the contents of the boiler being shot out towards the front and also partially along the tubes towards the back of the boiler.'*

Mr Sherwood: 'This particular accident was just as likely to have taken place on a bran-new boiler as in this?'

Witness: 'Yes, if the gauge was choked. The accident had nothing to with the age of the boiler.'

The Coroner: 'The explosion was not caused by corrosion or anything of that kind, but from the defective gauge?'

Witness: 'Yes. But for that the boiler would have lasted 20 years longer under good conditions.'

'Is there anything unusual in running a boiler of this kind for 24 years?'

'No, sir.'

The Coroner asked Mr Hawksley, of the firm of Hawksley, Wild, and Co., if he could throw any further light upon the matter. Did he agree with the report, read by Mr Hiller?

Mr Hawksley: 'I do entirely.'

The Coroner: 'And the evidence he has given in answer to the court?'

Witness: 'I quite agree with what Mr Hiller has said, and if it had not been for this accident, and the boiler had been well cared for it would have done for ten or twenty years.'

The Coroner: 'Is it possible that Lickfold could have allowed this accident without being guilty of extreme carelessness or foolishness or recklessness? Was he guilty of all those?'

Witness: 'I think he has been thoroughly mistaken in the height of his water through his not thoroughly testing his gauges.'

'Could he have worked safely with one gauge, the other being out of order?'

'Undoubtedly.'

The ended the official evidence.

The Coroner, in his summing up, said he had never known a case in the whole of his experience in which he had heard more reports with regard to the cause of the accident and the persons to blame for it.

The jury then returned a verdict of accidental death in relation to all the victims, who had all died as a result of injuries received by the explosion, which itself was as a result of a defective water gauge.

The site of Messrs Southern and Richardson, Doncaster Street, with Shepherd Street in the background and Ellis Street in the foreground. The current building, now out of use and boarded up, was most recently occupied by toolmakers Record Ridgeway (photograph 2012)

This devastating explosion in which seven people were killed occurred just fifty yards from and thirteen years after the Matthew Street wall collapse, in which eight children died. It will be noticed that one of the victims of the Matthew Street accident was seven-year-old Clifford Anderson, of Burnt Tree Lane, and one of the boys killed in 1899 was Frank Anderson, aged fifteen, of No.4 court, No.3 house, Burnt Tree Lane. They were brothers; a sad and unlikely coincidence.

CHAPTER 30

TWO DEATHS AT A SHEFFIELD BREWERY, 1900 AND 1853

'Stupefied with drink, he was unable to rouse himself'

Isaac Hornsey and his family moved to Sheffield from the Scarborough area in the late nineteenth century. Finding a place to live at No.43 Silver Street near the city centre, he took a job as an engine fitter. Later he moved to No.11 Bertha Street, between Infirmary Road and Penistone Road, and found employment at the Don Brewery on Penistone Road. It was to be the last job he had, for it was there that he died in unusual circumstances.

The *News of the World* of June 14, 1900 explains what happened to Isaac:

DEATH BY AMMONIA FUMES
Isaac Hornsey, 51, was employed at the Don Brewery, Sheffield, where his duties included the care of the refrigerator, which is charged with ammonia. In the early hours of the morning he opened the valve of the refrigerator and immediately afterwards accidentally dropped the key which fell through an opening in the floor, and could not be recovered at once. Fumes of ammonia began to fill the room and though Hornsey did his best to close the valve with a spanner, his efforts were unsuccessful and in a few minutes he was overcome and fell back unconscious. He died a few days later.

The Don Brewery on Penistone Road, Sheffield, in 1890

Ammonia was used widely as a coolant in the refrigeration units of the time. The late nineteenth century had seen major developments in the brewing industry. Temperature-controlled malting gave the finished beer more consistency and refrigeration aided beer production in the summer months. The Don Brewery had been in existence 72 years at the time of the accident. Founded in 1828 under the ownership of Warburton, Turton and Howe, it remained so until 1849 when it was acquired by William Smith and Joseph Redfern. Smith was already a wealthy man living in Barnes Hall, Ecclesfield, to the north of Sheffield. Redfern busied himself in the brewing process and the running of the business whilst Smith set about building up a tied estate. In the following twenty years they acquired 28 public houses and leased another six. Their sons, Alfred Harrison Smith and Joseph Redfern junior, joined the board and took over the running of the business. Redfern junior died in 1889, so Alfred Harrison Smith took over full control of the brewery. At the time of his death the estate stood at about 40 public houses. The business continued to expand and at the time of Alfred's retirement in 1900, the estate had more than doubled to 83. It had also become a public registered company just prior to Smith's retirement. Expansion continued into the twentieth century, albeit at a slower rate. By 1915, a further seventeen pubs had been added, bringing up the hundred. But with the Government of that great Liberal Lloyd George hankering to introduce prohibition, and because of uncertainty of business brought about the war in Europe, the shareholders accepted an offer from the Tennant Brothers for both the brewery and the tied estate.

The Don Brewery was sited at the junction of Penistone Road and Infirmary Road, more or less adjacent to St Philip's Church. Tennant's 'mothballed' the brewery until 1958, when parts were sold off on a piecemeal basis. Tennant's was amalgamated into Whitbread's in 1962. A Sheffield City Council road-widening scheme finished off the site soon afterwards. A stone (below) now on the site is a cast of the original plaster sign that disintegrated when removed. It stands on the old Penistone Road opposite the end of Green Lane, and is not visible from the new Penistone Road.

Silver Street, where Isaac Hornsey lived when he first moved to Sheffield, still exists, but is now occupied solely by modern buildings. Bertha Street, his next abode, was a dead end than ran off Wood Lane, which still exists. Bertha Street remained until the late 1960s, when the area was cleared of housing.

Isaac Hornsey was not the first man to meet his demise at the Don Brewery. Forty-seven years earlier there was a fatality in even more unlikely circumstances than those that caused Hornsey's death. The following report in the *Manchester Guardian*, dated April 13, 1853, refers to an incident that had occurred eight days earlier:

A MAN SMOTHERED IN MALT AT SHEFFIELD

A singular and fatal accident occurred early on Tuesday morning, the 5th inst., at the Don Brewery, Shalesmoor. The floor of a chamber, containing upwards of 200 quarters of malt, gave way in consequence of one of the beams snapping asunder, and a large portion of the contents were precipitated into an open shed beneath. The accident is supposed to have taken place at about four o'clock in the morning. Soon afterwards Mr Redfearn (Smith, Redfearn & Co.) was apprised of the accident, and on going into the shed he was surprised to see the legs of a man protruding from the outer edge of the malt, the upper part of the body being covered with malt. Life was quite extinct when the body was removed. It was conveyed to the New Inn, and there identified as that of James Johnson, a single man, aged 26. He was last seen alive late on Monday evening, being then in a state of intoxication. He appeared to have gone to lie down in this shed, and was asleep when the floor fell, and covered him with malt. Stupefied with drink, he was unable to rouse himself, else a slight exertion on his part would have been sufficient to rescue him. The occurrence was investigated by he coroner on Tuesday evening, and a verdict of 'accidental death' returned.

CHAPTER 31

MURDER AT THE MIDLAND STATION, 1900

'Hague fell to the ground, simply saying, "Oh"'

The Times of September 24, 1900 gave the following report:

MURDER IN SHEFFIELD.

Late on Saturday night a murder of a most brutal character was perpetrated in Sheffield, the victim being Walter Hague, of Cowley-lane, Chapeltown, near Sheffield. Hague, who was a planer engaged by Messrs. Newton, Chambers, and Co., of the Thorncliffe Iron Works, was about 23 years of age.

He has for some time been engaged to Miss Alice Basford, a barmaid at the Carlton Hotel, Sheffield, but the two had had a disagreement and had not seen each other for a considerable period until Saturday week. On that day they renewed their friendship and Hague promised to visit her at the hotel again on the following Saturday. This he did. He proceeded from Chapeltown, to Sheffield on Saturday night and waited until Miss Basford was relieved from her duties shortly after 11 o'clock. The lady resides at Darnall, one of the suburbs of the city, and the two walked towards the Midland Company's station. Sheaf Street, along which they passed, is not at all well lighted – on one side is a high wall, the boundary to the Midland Company's line, and on the other are works – and they came upon a man who appeared to be drunk before they had any idea he was there. Rain was falling at the time, and the couple were sheltering themselves under an umbrella. The man was swearing, but Hague and his lady companion took little notice of him, as they were pressed for time to catch their train. They walked along briskly, and had reached the entrance to the station used by the parcel vans when someone seized Hague and threw him to the ground. Almost before Miss Basford knew what had happened Hague's assailant had given him a violent kick and made off, but she saw sufficient of him to recognize him as the drunken fellow she had just passed. The injured man apparently thought very little was the matter with him, because he got up and, remarking that he wished a policeman had been at hand and he would have given the man in custody, he asked the young lady to knock the dirt from his clothes. This she was doing when Hague fell to the ground, simply saying, 'Oh.' Miss Basford at once summoned assistance.

Hague was removed to the Midland Station and placed on a barrow, and a medical man who was close at hand examined him. It was at once clear that Hague had been badly stabbed, and before anything could be done for him he died. The body was removed to the public mortuary, and an examination showed that with an ordinary pocket knife Hague had been stabbed in the region of the heart. Considerable force must have been used as the instrument had gone through a thick coat, waistcoat, shirt front, and vest, and had passed for a considerable distance into the flesh. Miss Basford states that she never saw a knife, but Hague must have been stabbed when his murderer was on the top of him on the ground. The murderer got clear away, and the police have no trace of him. The young lady says he was about 36 years of age and had the appearance of a working man, probably a collier dressed in his best clothes.

An inquest was held, but it could shed no further light on the affair. Hague was not known to have any quarrel with anyone and Miss Basford said there could be no question of jealousy. A verdict of wilful murder was returned against a person unknown. The *Illustrated Police News* reported: 'As for the murderer, he has disappeared utterly, and the police consider themselves baffled.' However, less than a month later there was a much unexpected development in the city of Hull. The *Manchester Times* of October 12, 1900 reported:

THE SHEFFIELD MURDER
A CONFESSION AT HULL
MARINE ENGINEER SURRENDERS HIMSELF

Between 11 and 12 o'clock Monday night a man giving the name of George Donovan went to the Parliament Street police station, Hull, and told the sergeant in charge that he had come to give himself up on the charge of murdering Walter Hague at Sheffield on the 27th September, and for which he was wanted by Sheffield police. He said he was a marine foreman and was 38 years old. He further stated that he had been in Hull about a week, seeking a berth on a ship, but had failed. In reply to interrogations he stated that he went from Hull to Sheffield on a visit, and met a woman with whom he became friendly. He bought her a hat or a bonnet and they intended to proceed to Hull together by the night train. He had a lot to drink but they proceeded towards the station quietly together. Suddenly he missed his companion and going as directly as he could to the Midland Station he thought that he saw the woman that was to accompany him in company with another man. He promptly went forward to renegotiate with her, whereupon her companion resented his intrusion and, as far as he could see, intended to follow it up with forcible methods. Upon this, and purely in self defence, and with no idea of doing serious injury to the man, he drew his knife and stabbed him. He lost his hat in the struggle and remained in Sheffield overnight. The prisoner then went on to state that he afterwards went on to Hull and the consciousness of the crime so worried him that he thought it would be best to give himself up to the authorities and have the matter put an end to.

Prisoner on Tuesday was taken to Sheffield. It is ascertained that the prisoner later seemed somewhat inclined to cast some doubt on his previous confession. He still adheres, however, to the statement that he remembers having an altercation, and that he made an attack on some person. The man James Donovan was brought up at the Sheffield Court House on Wednesday. The case was taken before the Stipendiary Magistrate and Donovan was charged with wilful murder, the information being laid before the Chief Constable Commander Scott. Various witnesses were examined and afterwards the prisoner made a statement denying his alleged confession, insisting that he was not sober when he made it, after which he was remanded.

Postcard of the Midland Station circa 1900 – the scene of the crime is just to the left of the station on Sheaf Street.

MYSTERIOUS MURDER IN SHEFFIELD.

Thirteen days later the same newspaper explained further:

THE SHEFFIELD MURDER
Donovan was perfectly sober at the time he made his statement, though he had been drinking some days previously. The prosecution, which was conducted on instructions from the Treasury, traced Donovan's movements in Sheffield up to half an hour before the murder, but after that nothing could be heard of him until next morning. The evidence of several persons who witnessed the tragedy was taken, and most of them agreed that Donovan was like the murderer, but none absolutely identified him. The prisoner was committed for trial at the Assizes.

Before Donavan's trial, Mr Justice Wright, at Leeds Assizes, stated to a Grand Jury that he believed although the man had been charged with murder, there was probably insufficient evidence to obtain a conviction for such a charge. He said there was considerable reason to think that the deceased man was the aggressor, and that would probably be sufficient to reduce the charge to one of manslaughter. However, the judge would leave the decision to the Grand Jury as to which charge Donovan would face at trial. The Grand Jury opted for a trial for murder, which was reported on by the *Sheffield and Rotherham Independent*:

THE SHEFFIELD MURDER
WHO STABBED WALTER HAGUE?
TRIAL AT LEEDS ASSIZES
The trial of James Donovan, ship's fireman, on the charge of murdering Walter Hague, at Sheffield, came on at the West Riding Assizes, Leeds, yesterday. The result of the trial tended, if anything, to intensify the mystery and doubt which has surrounded the dark crime of September 22nd from the first. As most people anticipated, the evidence against Donovan proved quite inadequate to uphold the capital charge. Not one of the numerous witnesses were able to identify him as the mysterious assailant, and the case collapsed like a house of cards before a single witness had been called on the prisoner's behalf. Donovan, who is 38 years of age, is a man under the average height, broad in the shoulders, and sturdily built, with pale complexion and dark hair and beard. He regarded the proceedings yesterday with the same stolidity that he has maintained throughout.

Mr Harold Thomas, with Mr Felix Palmer, prosecuted for the Crown, and Mr J. A. Slater (instructed by Mr P. B. Richardson) defended prisoner. Mr Thomas, in opening the case, made a full recital of the circumstances surrounding the murder, and said that the questions for the jury were: Was the prisoner the man who stabbed Hague, and if so, were the circumstances such as to amount to wilful murder, or only manslaughter? The prosecution relied upon the statements of certain persons who saw the stabbing done, and also upon the prisoner's own statements after the murder. The prisoner was a seafaring man, and on the 22nd September he was in Sheffield seeing some friends. On the evening of that day, Hague, who was an iron worker, in the employ of Messrs Newton, Chambers and Co., Chapeltown, was walking towards the Midland Station with a young woman named Alice Basford, intending to catch a train at half-past eleven. At the bottom of Commercial Street they passed a man who was talking to himself, and apparently cursing some unknown person. The prosecution suggested that this man, who was drunk, was the prisoner. Hague and Miss Basford proceeded along Sheaf Street, and when they reached the lower station gates, Hague was seized from behind by a man. A cabman, who was driving past, saw a flash of a bright instrument, and Hague was stabbed and fell to the ground. His assailant ran off. Hague died almost immediately after being wounded. He had one wound in front of the throat, and another between the third and fourth ribs, which pierced the heart.

Two days afterwards the Sheffield police arrested Donovan on suspicion, but ultimately he was released. On the night of the murder Donovan was seen in the Bay Horse Inn, Greystock Street, from eight o'clock to half-past ten. Shortly before eleven he purchased a hat in Westbar, saying that he had lost his other in a row. He was seen in Sheaf Street about a quarter-past eleven. After his release by the Sheffield police Donovan was next heard of a fortnight later, when he went to the police station at Hull and made a voluntary statement. Donovan's subsequent statement before the magistrates was that he went to the police station to 'explain the matter and stop people talking'. He also asserted that he was drunk when he saw the Hull police, and that the police knew he was not in a proper condition to make a statement. He also said that the police cross-questioned him continually all night, and never allowed him to sleep. Next morning, when the police told him that he had confessed, he said that he came to explain, not to confess. This was denied by the police.

The first witness was Police Constable Hargreaves, of the Hull Police Force, who said that on October 8th, at eleven at night, the prisoner came to the police station. He was then perfectly sober, and made a statement which was taken down in writing, and signed by him. He *stated that he was wanted in Sheffield for murder. Asked when it took place he replied, 'About a fortnight ago last Saturday.' He further stated that they could not do anything to him because they had had him once for it. Two policemen apprehended him at the Victoria Railway Station on the following Monday, and detained him for four or five hours. He further stated that he had stabbed the man near to the railway station, and that he lost his hat in the struggle and went into a shop and bought another. He said that he left Hull on the morning of the murder for Sheffield, and got into company with a young woman. 'I bought her a new hat,' prisoner's statement went on, 'and another man got the woman away from me, and I could not put up with it, so I struck him with my knife and ran away. Since I was detained in Sheffield I have been troubled a great deal about it, and have talked about it in my sleep. I was afraid that someone would give me away, so I thought I would make a clean breast of it.'*

Miss Alice Basford, who is employed at the Carlton Restaurant, High Street, was the next witness. She described once more how, as she was going towards the station with Hague, a man came up behind, put his arms around Hague's neck, and threw him to the ground. The man immediately ran away towards Howard Street. She raised Hague to his feet, but he dropped down again, and died almost at once.

Mr Harold Thomas: 'Did you notice the man?'

Miss Basford: 'I only had a passing look at him as we passed him at the bottom of Granville Hill. I didn't think anything about him at the time.'

'Did you see the prisoner at the police station on the 9th October, among other men?'

'I picked that man out as well as I could from the description of him.'

'I suppose there is not the slightest truth in the suggestion that you have met this man before?'

'No, not to my knowledge.'

'For instance, he had never bought you a hat?'

'No, certainly not.'

In answer to further questions, Miss Basford said there was no struggle before Hague was struck. He did not cry out for assistance. She did not notice whether the assailant had a beard or not, but she saw that he had a dark moustache and a sallow complexion.

Gertrude Gulson, a young girl, said that she was going with her sister to the Midland Station on the Saturday night. She saw 'one man knock the other down'. The man who struck Hague was wearing a stiff hat, black jacket and waistcoat, and blue trousers. She did not notice anything else.

Mr Slater: 'You didn't see the man's face?'

Witness: 'No.'

Miss Basford was recalled by the Judge, and repeated her statement that nothing took place between the men before Hague was struck to the ground. Arthur Houlgate, the cab driver who drove past with his cab at the moment of the murder, said he saw a man put his arm round Hague's neck and strike him. Witness saw the flash of some bright instrument in the assailant's hand. Witness's attention was drawn to the occurrence by hearing a scream.

Mr Slater: 'You took so little notice of it that you went on with your fare to the station?'

Witness: 'Yes.'

Edith Gulson, who was passing with her sister on the way to the station, said that hearing a noise she turned round and saw Hague on the floor. Hague got up, and the other man then struck him again. In reply to Mr Slater, witness said it was a dark night, and raining slightly. She only noticed that the man who struck Hague was dark, and not very tall. She could not say whether he wore a beard or not. His Lordship (interposing): 'What is the good of all this if none of the witnesses identify him?'

Arthur George Walker, waiter at the Carlton Restaurant, arrived on the scene after the murder had been committed. He said that Hague was lying on the ground, and Miss Basford asked him to run after a man who had been striking him. Annie Frow, of Masborough, gave somewhat remarkable evidence. She was passing, and saw the attack upon Hague. She said to Hague, 'Why don't you hit him back?' The assailant said to her, 'Would you hit him back?' He was a big-built man, fair, wearing a brown coat, dark trousers, and a dark cap. He had no beard, and if he had a moustache, it was so fair that she did not notice it.

Mr Slater (pointing to the prisoner): 'Is that the man?'

191

Witness: 'No, that is not the man. I never saw him before I was taken to see him at the police station.'

Mr Thomas: 'Can you tell me what the complexion of the deceased man was?'

'I think his hair was dark. I paid more attention to the man who was running away.'

William A. Sullivan, landlord of the Bay Horse Inn, Greystock Street, said that Donovan was sober when he left his house on Saturday night. Mr Harold Thomas, in reply to the Judge, said that if Donovan's confession at Hull could not be relied on. He, therefore, did not intend to proceed further with the case against Donovan. His Lordship said that the jury could not possibly be asked to convict upon the evidence before them. It looked very much like a case in which a man who had been in drink had heard, or perhaps even seen, something happen, and then got into such a mood that he made a confession to the police. The jury accordingly returned a verdict of 'Not guilty'. Donovan was discharged.

What is not made clear in the reports is why the police arrested and questioned Donovan two days after the assault, and why he was released four or five hours later. Regardless of Donovan's 'confession', which he later retracted, the conflicting witness statements made it impossible for him to be convicted. He was wearing a stiff hat; he was wearing a dark cap. He was not very tall; he was big-built. He had a dark moustache; if he had a moustache it was too fair to be seen. He had dark hair; he had fair hair. He had a beard; it was not noticed that he had a beard. He was wearing a black jacket; he was wearing a brown coat. He was wearing dark trousers; he was wearing blue trousers. So William Hague's killer, whether or not it was Donovan, escaped punishment.

EPILOGUE

In the modern era, official crime statistics published by the Home Office perennially show that Sheffield fares favourably when compared with other large towns and cities. For example, in 1999, Manchester had one of the highest overall crime rates outside London. Sheffield, similar in size and social background and just 35 miles away over the Pennines, did not. Indeed, the BBC reported that Sheffield was 'the safest of the big cities'. When it came to violent offences against the person, in 1999 the numbers implied that Sheffield was more than four times safer than Manchester.

These were not isolated or freak statistics; similar figures from 2008 and 2009 placed Sheffield better than Leicester, Nottingham, Manchester, Bristol, London, Birmingham, Liverpool and Leeds for all aspects of rates of crime. In the period 2010-2011, the national average for violent crimes against the person was 14.8 offences per 1,000 population. Sheffield's average was a mere 10.9, one of the few large cities to fall below the national average (the others were Leeds 14.5; Swansea 14.2; Sunderland 12.9; York 12.6; Gloucester 12.4; Bradford 12.0; Dover 11.8). Every major city had worse crime rates than Sheffield, with Southampton topping the charts with 31.6 offences per thousand population. Other selected figures were: London 25.4; Nottingham 22.8; Manchester 22.3; Hull 21.9; Birmingham 17.9; Liverpool 16.3; Newcastle 15.1.

Despite the statistics, murders and violent crime seem to dominate the front pages of the local Sheffield press with alarming regularity, and figures such as those above must always be viewed with a degree of suspicion as to their reliability and accuracy, but the unavoidable conclusion is that, just as in

1999, Sheffield remains one of the 'safest' cities in England and Wales in which to live; in relation to some it is so by a fair distance. It may not be 'four times safer than Manchester', as it was supposed to be in 1999, but it could be argued that it is more than twice as safe.

But has this state of affairs always been the case? Using the formation of the London Metropolitan Police in 1829 as a starting point, it is hard to say, partly because relevant statistics are not easy to come by, and partly because even the scarce figures that are available might not have employed uniform standards of measurement and analysis. For example, up to the 1930s, the police in some parts of the country routinely recorded thefts as 'lost property', and, particularly in Victorian times, what were termed the 'criminal classes' of society did not have trust or faith in, or respect for, the police, so countless crimes were not reported.

The London Metropolitan Police first maintained crime statistics as early as 1847, from which they were able to identify patterns of crimes and any possible connection between them. This methodical approach formed the basis of modern detective work. Police forces were established throughout the country by the mid 1850s and were subject to Parliamentary inspection, and alongside more efficient policing stood a strict judiciary, which was severe in its punishment of crimes and behaviour that the Victorians considered offensive. Up to 1868 this punishment could include transportation to Australia for those guilty of particularly outrageous offences, though this option was seldom enforced by the courts after the early 1850s. But the application of punishment varied in different cities. In April 1868, Alfred Aspland, a letter writer to the *Manchester Guardian*, complained that his home city, Manchester, was failing in its duties in this regard. According to him, only six per cent of serious crime in Manchester was punished, whereas in London it was 22 per cent, in Birmingham 36 per cent, in Leeds 45 per cent, but in Sheffield 53 per cent. The Sheffield law-enforcers could certainly not be similarly accused.

Before the advent of an organised police force in Sheffield, according to an 1833 report in the *Yorkshire and Derbyshire Advertiser* one might assume that such a body was hardly required. During the first week in March of that year the Magistrates dealt with a grand total of three crimes; two for petty theft and one man imprisoned because he 'had no worse character than that of a vagrant'. The following week the Magistrates were less busy; they had just a single case before them, that of 'an idle boy charged with neglecting his work'. At that time the population of the Sheffield district stood at 114,000, so, if official figures are to be believed, Sheffield was an incredibly safe and crime-free place. However, the report concluded with a caveat: 'during the last six days, the constables have been absent from the town attending the Assizes at York'. How many constables were so occupied was not disclosed, but perhaps the negligible amount of work the Magistrates had to perform was more due to the fact that in the absence of the constables the local population could get away with anything, rather than that they were all law-abiding citizens.

Three decades later, on November 7, 1865, the *Manchester Guardian* published details of what must have been one of the first nationwide surveys of criminal activity in a report entitled 'Comparative Criminality of Manufacturing and Commercial Towns':

> *A cursory inspection of publications might lead anyone to suppose that we possess in this country means as ample for testing the moral circumstances of our cities and towns, as for estimating their sanitary conditions. The Registrar General furnishes the health criterion; the 'Judicial Statistics' of the Home Office should supply us with a test of the relative criminality of different districts of the kingdom. We are acquainted through the returns, among a multitude of other important matters, with the number of criminal classes in each town; the number of houses which are known to be the habitual resort of thieves, receivers, and prostitutes; the number and character of the crimes annually reported to the local police; the total number of persons apprehended; the number charged with the graver crimes and offences who are committed to trial; the number who for lighter misdeeds are summarily convicted by the magistrates; the number who were so convicted for drunken and disorderly conduct and for common assaults; and, if we are inclined to be discursive in our research, we may trace the offenders, with all their penal incidents, through many pages bristling with figures.*

> *The places selected for comparison are some of the chief seats of the cotton and woollen trade, of mixed textile production, of iron, hardware and cutlery trade; to these are added one principal and three or four minor seaport and commercial towns. In the aggregate, our list represents, according to the last census, a population approaching to three millions souls (2,741,000). To give a sufficient basis, the criminal statistics have been taken on the average of the last six years ended with 1863. The last enumeration of the inhabitants of these towns was effected in the middle of this period, i.e. in the early part of 1861. The*

census may, therefore, be fairly taken as representing the mean population of the whole period.

It requires nearly 4,000 men as a police force to keep the dangerous classes in these towns under more or less efficient check. The precise ratio to the inhabitants generally is 1.4 per 1,000.

The proportion varied greatly in different towns; Sheffield had one policeman per thousand population, with Manchester and Liverpool requiring more than twice as many. The reason for this disparity, according to the *Manchester Guardian*, was because of the 'Irish problem':

Lancashire has attracted an enormous amount of Irish labour to her towns, and this has had a marked influence upon her criminal calendar. The Irish-born portion of the inhabitants of England forms only 3 per cent, yet so great is their disposition to transgress, that 15 per cent of the inmates of English prisons are Irish.

At the time the population of Manchester was eleven per cent Irish, that of Liverpool ten per cent Irish, but that of Birmingham just four per cent Irish.

Next, the report detailed the 'Number of criminal class known to the police in each town, average of the six years ended with 1863'. This section showed that Sheffield possessed just 3.5 'criminal class' inhabitants per thousand, whereas the figures for Wolverhampton and Birmingham were 16.2 and 16.3 respectively; they must have been particularly dreadful places. Of the twenty towns surveyed just Stockport was better in this category than Sheffield.

Now the survey concentrated on 'bad houses', or 'houses for receiving stolen goods; public houses, beershops, &c., the resort of thieves and prostitutes, brothels and houses of ill-fame; tramps' lodging houses'. Once more, Sheffield did comparatively well, its proportion of 'rendezvous of the criminal classes' being small (one per thousand), with only Stockport and Oldham faring better. Wolverhampton (4.2) and Hull (4.0) headed the table.

The next statistic studied was the 'Number of crimes indictable, average of the six years ended with 1863', with Sheffield (2.5 per thousand) again in the top five. The worst was Manchester (18.1 per thousand).

Unfortunately, these Home Office 'Judicial Statistics' did not dissect crimes into offences of various natures, so it is impossible to deduce how many were violent offences, how many were petty theft, how many were sexual assault etc. Regardless, what can be deduced is that in the mid 1860s Sheffield required fewer policemen, had a smaller proportion of its population as members of the 'criminal classes', had fewer houses of ill repute, and was less prevalent to unlawful and illicit activity than a large sample of other industrial towns.

In November 1872 the *Sheffield and Rotherham Independent* gave an insight into the types and numbers of crimes committed in Sheffield, comparing that year with a decade earlier. The report detailed numbers of indictable crimes and their frequency in relation to the number of inhabitants of the city according to the 1861 and 1871 Censuses. In that time the population of Sheffield had increased from 185,157 to 239,941. The statistics, provided by the Central Police Offices, suggested that violent crimes were few and overall crime had in fact fallen in relation to the total population in the preceding ten years: one crime per 450 people in 1862 and one per 535 people in 1872. These numbers are tiny compared with modern standards; in the mid 2000s the number of notifiable offences in Sheffield reached some 67,000 annually.

However, from the scant evidence of the mid-Victorian period and the more complete statistics of 21st century Britain, it may be fairly argued – though not conclusively – that Sheffield was, and still is, a relatively 'safe' place amongst similarly sized towns and cities. That is certainly the case today, and if this was also the case in 1865, perhaps it has always been so. But then how can one explain away the many heinous acts described in the chapters of this book? They cannot be explained; there have always been and there will always be individuals who are so overtaken by envy, wrath, revenge or greed that they take the life of another human being, no matter what the time period, no matter what the location. It may not seem so, but fortunately such individuals are, and were, few and far between.

BIBLIOGRAPHY

Books

Bentley, David (2003); *Sheffield Murders, 1865-1965*, ALD Design and Print, Sheffield

Heeley History Workshop (2004); *Heeley and Thereabouts: Work, Play and People*, Pickard Communication, Sheffield

Hey, David (1998); *A History of Sheffield*, Carnegie Publishing Ltd, Lancaster

Lamb, Douglas (1996); *A Pub On Every Corner*, Hallamshire Publications Ltd, Sheffield

Machan, Peter (2000); *Lost Sheffield: Portrait of a Victorian City*, ALD Design and Print, Sheffield

Senior, Joseph (2008); *Smithy Rhymes and Stithy Chimes: Or the Short and Simple Annals of the Poor, Spelt by the Unlettered Muse of Your Humble Bard*, Kessinger Publishing, Whitefish, Massachusetts

Stockman, Rocky (1993); *The Hangman's Diary: A Calendar of Judicial Hangings*, Headline Book Publishing, London

Newspapers, Magazines, Journals and Periodicals

Birmingham Daily Post

Daily News

Derby Mercury

Hull Packet and East Riding Times

Illustrated Police Gazette

Illustrated Police News

Illustrated Police Review

Leeds Mercury

Liverpool Mercury

Lloyds Weekly Newspaper

Manchester Guardian

Manchester Times

News of the World

Police Gazette

Preston Chronicle

Sheffield and Rotherham Independent

Sheffield Daily Telegraph

Sheffield Times

The Era

The Globe

The Scotsman

The Times

Western Mail

York Herald

Yorkshire and Derbyshire Advertiser

Websites

www.chrishobbs.com/

www.capitalpunishmentuk.org/

www.historyandpolicy.org/

www.wikipedia.org/

www.sheffieldhistory.co.uk

www.bbc.co.uk

http://www.upmystreet.com/local/crime-in-sheffield.html

http://emedicine.medscape.com/article/1072987-overview

Other Sources

Official Census Records

Sheffield Local Register

Free BMD Register

Royal Commission on Capital Punishment

Old Ordnance Survey Maps published by Alan Godfrey Maps, Consett: Grenoside 1901; Sheffield (North) 1905; Sheffield (Loxley Valley) 1902; Sheffield (West) 1903; Sheffield 1903; Sheffield (Heeley) 1903; Sheffield (Neepsend) 1903; Ecclesall & Sharrow 1903; Nether Edge 1903.

ABOUT THE AUTHORS

Chris Hobbs was born in Sheffield and has lived in the city all his life. After a chequered career that has involved stints as a milkman, machinist, bank clerk, manager, support officer and technician, he became the holder of the domain name *www.chrishobbs.com* in 2002. Originally a family history site, it now also contains many articles that have a Sheffield connection. This is Chris's first book.

Matthew Bell is also Sheffield born and bred. A mechanical engineer by trade, he spends his every spare moment writing, and has a keen interest in football and local history. He has edited the Sheffield United FC fanzine *Flashing Blade* for over twenty years and has written a weekly column in the *Green 'Un* sportspaper since 1993. His latest work, *Red, White and Khaki – The Story of the Only Wartime FA Cup Final*, published in 2011, studied the impact on the country – and on Sheffield in particular – of the continuation of professional football during the first year of the Great War.

In 2010, with Dr Gary Armstrong, he co-authored *Fit and Proper? Conflicts and Conscience in an English Football Club*, the definitive account of the recent history of Sheffield United FC. He was co-editor of *Blades Tales* and *Blades Tales 2* and has written articles for *4-4-2* magazine, the 2003 Sheffield United v Arsenal FA Cup semi-final programme and Yorkshire County Cricket Club.

MYSTERIOUS MURDER IN SHEFFIELD.